Versatile Selling

WILSON LEARNING LIBRARY

Versatile Selling

Adapting your style so customers say "*YES!*"

How to order: single copies may be ordered online at www.novavistapub.com.
In North America, you may phone 1-503-548-7597. Elsewhere, dial +32-14-21-11-21.

ISBN 978-90-77256-03-9

D/2007/9797/2

Printed and bound in the United States of America.

20 19 18 17 16 15 14 13 12 11 10 9 8

Cover design: Bright Art Design
Text design: Layout Sticker

Contents

Foreword

Versatile Selling is not so much about selling something to people, but rather helping people sell something to themselves. In this case, the *something* they're buying is you.

You've probably heard that the apple seldom falls far from the tree, so it won't surprise you to know that my father was a great salesperson. He once told me his secret of success. "You can't sell your enemies, only your friends. So make everyone your friend." That's what will happen when you internalize the message in this book.

Versatile Selling gets below the surface and into the depths of why people like you, trust you, and want to do business with you – or why they don't.

If you've ever wondered how to connect with customers and others with more depth, breadth, and quality, this book is for you. Why? It will give theory and words to what you already know, but keep forgetting, in the daily battle for your share of life's rewards.

And by the way: If you read the previous sentence carefully and you were bothered by it, you're in luck. As the saying goes, when the student is ready, the book shows up.

Too often, we look at our relationships with customers and others as a fight, a competition for life's rewards. Yet we don't usually like people who compete with us, nor do they like us when we compete with them. We like people who cooperate with us, who share our dreams, fears, and aspirations. Above all, we like people who we feel understand us.

Stick this on your bathroom mirror: "80 percent of success in sales is having people believe that *you* understand *them*!"

Think back to a time when you had that great feeling of clicking with a new customer. You knew you could just be yourself, effortlessly. Your interaction felt natural, relaxed. You were more than just comfortable, you were "in the zone."

Chances are good that you and your new customer shared expectations of how people should *be* with each other. How you'd like to be treated by everyone. In the words of this book, you had similar Social

Styles. This means that your natural behavior patterns matched, and it freed you both to focus on what brought you together.

Now think about meeting a customer who seemed difficult, right from the start. You missed that sense of comfort, and you were not sure how to build trust and good feelings – you were on the defensive. It was harder for you to like this person, because this person wasn't "like" you.

It might unnerve you to know that this person, who is not "like" you, represents 75 percent of the population, 75 percent of the people you are trying to do business with, and 75 percent of the people you want to like you and buy from you.

But this book isn't only about differing Social Styles – it's about Versatility. It's one thing to know about the differences of another culture, but it's another to comfortably live within that culture as if it were your own. That's true Versatility. You learn to appreciate differences, adapt to them, and make the most of them.

This book turns the Golden Rule inside out and upside down. Treating people the way WE want to be treated can be wrong 75 percent of the time, and right only 25 percent!

Treating people the way THEY want to be treated, however, can be 100 percent right and effective. You could call this the Platinum rule. Everyone knows that ounce for ounce, platinum is worth more than gold – "Do unto others as they would have you do unto them."

And here's the hard part, but the part that makes it all work. Versatility is your willingness to get out of your comfort zone in order to keep others in their comfort zones.

Versatility is not an idea; it's a competency with three parts – attitude, knowledge and skill.

Read this book with the attitude of a learner who really does want to know how to create and sustain relationships that last – real win-win relationships. Devour the knowledge contained in these pages. Turn that knowledge into a skill and keep practicing it. If you do that, your Versatility will shine through and your success will be assured. You'll learn to like who you are and help others to like you more as well.

So, think V for Victory and for your Versatility . . . and savor the rewards it will bring you!

Larry Wilson

Social Style and Versatility

ANALYTICAL
- Focus on facts and logic
- Act when payoff is clear
- Careful not to commit too quickly

DRIVER
- Focus on results
- Take charge
- Make quick decisions
- Like challenges

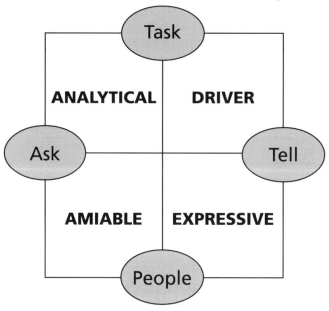

AMIABLE
- Cooperate to gain agreement
- Provide support
- Communicate trust and confidence

EXPRESSIVE
- Create excitement and involvement
- Share ideas, dreams, enthusiasm
- Motivate, inspire, persuade

Research and profiles of more than two million people around the world by Wilson Learning indicate that people fall into one of four Social Styles in terms of their comfort zones of behavior. Roughly 25 percent of the population falls into each group.

1 | The Number 1 Secret of Sales

Do not do unto others as you would that they should do unto you.
Their tastes may be different.
GEORGE BERNARD SHAW

There is a simple-but-profound truth about sales that has changed the lives and improved the fortunes of many salespeople throughout the world: Versatility sells. The ability to genuinely and strategically adapt your personal style can lead to amazing things when it comes to moving customers to say "Yes."

Don't misunderstand. Simple does not mean easy. Versatility requires a combination of skill, awareness and adaptability that can test the limits of even the most seasoned salesperson. If you sell for your livelihood you know what it means to deal with rejection every day. Yet most of us still don't deliberately head into places and situations that make us uneasy. That is precisely where *Versatile Selling* will lead you, however, because research and real-world experience show success in sales starts with making your customers comfortable. Your comfort is secondary.

Customer comfort is the essence of Versatility. Assuring your customer's comfort will pay off in many ways. Among other things, it will help you get better quality information to help shape your solution, stronger customer support for your sales process, and establish critically important foundations for a long-term relationship.

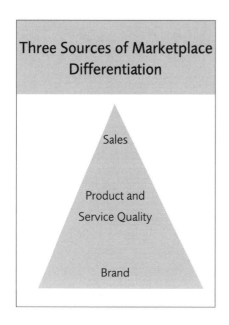

Three Sources of Marketplace Differentiation

Sales

Product and Service Quality

Brand

THE DIMINISHING POWER OF BRAND AND QUALITY

Why is Versatility so important? Because it might be one of the few sources of competitive advantage left to salespeople. Let's take a look at how this has evolved.

There was a time when products and services could almost sell themselves. A strong brand identity could open many doors for a competent salesperson. Name recognition alone could often cause buyers to overlook significant shortcomings in a relationship with a product or service provider. It happened when IBM introduced its first microcomputers in the early 1980s.

The IBM name was recognized worldwide because of its dominance in the mainframe computer market. Steve Jobs and Steve Wozniak get credit for starting the microcomputer revolution when they built the first Apple computer in a garage in California, but the power of the IBM brand was critical, not only to IBM's initial entry into this market but to the success of the entire fledgling industry. This new technology needed early adopters willing to pay a high price and face a steep learning curve in order to get a foothold in the market. The IBM name provided legitimacy and promised longevity at a time when skepticism was strong. Ken Olson, then president of mini- and mainframe computer maker Digital Equipment Corp., is widely quoted as saying, "There is no reason for any individual to have a computer in his home."

But the IBM brand eased computers into the workplace and then into homes with remarkable speed. With time, IBM's Brand power diminished in the face of growing competition. Today the major players (among them Dell, Compaq, Fujitsu, Gateway, Toshiba, Hewlett-Packard and others) are all more or less equivalent from a Brand perspective.

Another source of competitive advantage, product and service quality, is also disappearing. Quality was once enough to almost guarantee strong sales. There was a period in North America in the late 1980s and early 1990s, for example, when the influence of total quality management, which gained worldwide attention because of its widespread applications in Japan, meant Toyotas, Hondas and other Japanese cars would outsell those built domestically. Consumers believed the imported vehicles were better, would last longer and have fewer maintenance problems. The efficiencies that total quality management brought to the manufacturing process also helped hold down costs. *Better and cheaper* was a combination many buyers couldn't resist.

But, even with the powerful combination of brand identity and product and service quality IBM and the Japanese automakers brought to the market, their domination couldn't last.

Given the global, hypercompetitive marketplace in which we now live, it is only a matter of time before success attracts new hungry and clever competitors.

Competition can come from anywhere in the world. And, in large part because of the affordability and widespread availability of new technology, competitors can come from inside or outside your own industry. Think about what Dell Computers has done to the major players in the computer sales business. No company worldwide sells more home and business computers than Dell. It is a company started by a kid selling equipment out of his college dormitory room.

As a result of this ever-intensifying and creative competition, brand identity and product or service quality are essential. But they are now merely the minimum requirements for getting a potential customer's attention, the initial price for admission into the market. They are no longer enough to distinguish between competitors, and they certainly are not enough to guarantee sales.

THE BEST WAY TO DISTINGUISH YOURSELF FROM YOUR COMPETITORS

The third source of potential market differentiation, if brand and quality are no longer key differentiators, is what *you* do as a salesperson. It's what happens during the sales process. It's you.

As you no doubt have seen, however, many organizations focus instead on the strategic and competitive aspects of selling their products and services in their efforts to distinguish themselves. They adjust and readjust pricing. They overhaul marketing campaigns. They hire new advertising agencies. They spend millions to show commercials during the sports championships or to sponsor banner ads on the Internet. They create sexy incentive plans and rebates for their customers. They increase research-and-development investments to come up with new features for mature products. The resources and human effort devoted to these approaches are supporting entire industry sectors in their own right.

In the end, the organizations that focus primarily on strategic and competitive issues miss their single greatest opportunity to build sales.

They fail to see and to act on the tested fact that improving personal relationships with their customers and prospective customers is the best way to win business – by winning their trust. They think about strategy and competitive advantage and neglect the interpersonal skills of their sales force. These skills form the foundation of great customer relationships, and Versatility is the cornerstone for them.

It's quite simple: When it comes to finally making or not making a sale, it is often the salesperson's ability to sell differently to different customers that distinguishes the big winners.

That's Versatility in sales. That's your opportunity to move more of your customers to "Yes."

OUTRAGEOUS EXPECTATIONS?

We operate in a global marketplace in which buyers can and do expect salespeople to bend to their every quirk and unique need. And since

The Golden Rule Needs Bending

Bob Davis has learned firsthand the lesson playwright, author and philosopher George Bernard Shaw shared some hundred years ago when he said, *"Do not do unto others as you would that they should do unto you.* Their tastes may be different." As a senior associate with McCourt Associates, a Wilson Learning partner company, he has learned the lesson by selling and teaching others to sell using Versatility. "It has always been important to me to build relationships and demonstrate to customers how much I care about them," Davis says. "But early in my career the more I sold – and didn't sell – the more I realized I couldn't accomplish those goals the same way with every customer.

"I like to create a lot of color and splash with my written proposals to customers. I used to create personalized binders with artistic covers and rainbow-colored tabs for every project. It was one of my ways of putting my personality into my work. The lesson that I needed to be more versatile, however, hit me hard in Southern California one day when I handed over one of my 'works of art,' expecting an enthusiastic response. Instead, my client slowly and mechanically opened the binder, unsnapped the retaining rings, lifted out the contents, placed them on the desk, shut the binder and handed it back to me, saying, 'You can use this for someone else.'

"I was offended. Other customers loved my proposals. How could he do that?

"I figured out that he could do that because I was treating him the way I would want to be treated, not the way he wanted to be treated. I had misread him. He was the kind of person who seldom showed any kind of emotion. In all our meetings he always wanted to get right down to business. No small talk. He would frequently ask me for documentation to support my statements. He just wanted the facts. The colored binder was irrelevant, and, in fact, caused tension between us.

"There are four Social Styles, not just my own. The statistics tell us that 75 percent of the population is not like you in its Social Style. So, the Golden Rule as we've all learned it – *'Do unto others as you would have others do unto you'* – is the right way to go in terms of style only about 25 percent of the time.

"Versatility means, *'Do unto others as they would have you do unto them.'*"

buying smart has emerged as a critical success factor in every industry, this is not a whimsical or temporary situation.

As a customer yourself you may not even be conscious of this development, but much of the pain you feel when a sales situation does not go well is tied into customers' personal expectations. Thanks to the Internet and other research resources, customers today can be intimately well informed about what they want to buy. Thanks to competition, they have more options. Although we all deal with the occasional customer who makes us want to scream and believe otherwise, buyers today are generally more strategic and savvy.

The average customers may never directly say to you, "Adapt your selling style to match my buying style or I will shop with someone else who will." If you are aware of the signals, however, that attitude is often clear in their actions. The biggest challenge is that customers are like snowflakes – no two are identical. And no customer is exactly like you.

All of this is why Versatility is so critical to success in sales. Outrageous expectations, well met, are a sale most likely made.

A SELLING TOOL FOR TOUGH TIMES

The bottom line: Even though everybody you sell to may be buying the same product or service, you can't sell the same way to every customer. That may be a lesson you are learning the hard way, if you use the same basic sales presentation or approach with all your customers and are wondering why it works brilliantly with some and is an utterly painful failure with others.

Versatility is a rational response to this challenge to recognize and react to what may seem like puzzling or extreme demands. It is a conscious decision on your part to adapt your behaviors and approach in order to accommodate the personal preferences, priorities and buying styles of your customers.

Versatile Selling is based on the successful, proven Social Styles communication tool developed by Wilson Learning. In the past 40 years, more than *two million* people have learned about Social Styles and a million have learned about Versatility as it applies to sales worldwide. As you work your way through this book, you will learn about the four Social Styles. You will learn about your own Social Style and how it influences your success in sales. You will learn how to "read" your customer's preferred style. Finally, and most important, you will learn how to adapt your normal behaviors to sell better, taking into account the particular Social Style of your customer.

You have learned enough already that you probably won't be able to look at a customer "the same old way" again. That's a good sign that you're well on your way to Versatility, but read on. There's a lot more learning ahead that will help you create more comfort for your customers – and win more sales for you.

2 | The Foundations of Versatility

*After all, when you come right down to it,
how many people speak the same language
even when they speak the same language?*

RUSSELL HOBAN

The secrets of *Versatile Selling*, in their most elemental sense, center on behavior, language, communication and connection on the personal level. We'll reveal all in this chapter.

Versatile Selling is tied to behavior and language because there are a few key concepts you must understand to tap into the power of adapting your selling behaviors to accommodate people with different Social Styles. Concepts such as comfort, tension, assertiveness, responsiveness, relating, discovering, advocating and supporting are at the core of this power.

Versatile Selling is tied to communication and connection because sales don't happen without trust and confidence between buyer and seller. E-mail, cell phones, websites, palm-sized computers and an unending parade of new technological tools continue to change the face of business around the planet. We can bombard each other with information from an almost inescapable array of sophisticated communication tools. Many experts argue, however, that human interaction ultimately plays the most critical role in putting signatures on the dotted lines of sales agreements.

Depending on your own Social Style, right now you may be (1) Feeling eager to delve deeper into these terms, or (2) Feeling an urgent desire to move ahead to the chapters that will teach you specific tactics and techniques for selling more effectively.

Trust us on this. Spending the time to understand the terms that underlie the secrets of *Versatile Selling* is an important first step.

COMFORT – IT'S THEIRS THAT MATTERS, NOT YOURS

Success in sales is directly related to making customers comfortable.

We can't oversimplify or overlook the basics. To compete for a customer's attention, you must have an effective sales process, and you must be selling a product or service with a real value. But if there is a single defining characteristic that distinguishes the most successful salespeople, it is their ability to put people at ease. It is their capacity to help customers feel confident about their buying decisions, see the value of the product or service being purchased and feel the justifiability of the investment. This allows the customer to value, appreciate and anticipate the prospects of long-term satisfaction from the relationship.

Comfort in this context, of course, is a relative term. If you are selling cordless telephones in a retail electronics shop in the UK, comfort will probably come rather easily for your customers. The costs and the risks are relatively small. Comfort will likely be much more difficult to achieve, however, if you are selling multimillion-dollar legal services to multinational companies that have to abide by increasingly complex financial reporting standards.

Comfort for every customer will require different things from you. That, of course, is where things can get a bit perplexing. You might think if your customer is content, satisfied and feeling hopeful, that you should feel the same way. But it won't always work that way. In fact, it usually won't.

There are four main Social Styles that you will learn about in the

Versatility Creates Comfort – for the Customer

Marilyn Smith, a facilitator based in Toledo, Ohio who works with Wilson Learning in the US, tells this tale of comfort and conflict in behind-the-scenes sales planning. "Some time ago I was working with two colleagues, Scott and Tom, putting together a very detailed informational notebook about a client. The purpose of the notebook was to collect all our accumulated knowledge of the client's business issues, our history of working together, profiles of the client contacts including each contact's Social Style, and potentials for expanding the business. This book would be used to bring a new team up to speed on this client.

"Scott and I were arguing over how the book should be laid out. Scott said, 'It makes the most sense to start with where we are today with the client so the new team gets the picture quickly. Then we can let the rest of the detail follow.'"

"I replied, 'I disagree. We should start at the beginning and end with where we were today. Then the team will really see how we got here.'

"We were at an impasse. Tom finally interrupted us, laughing, and said, 'I think this is a style issue. Scott, you're a Driver, so you feel comfortable when the bottom line comes first. Marilyn, you're an Expressive, so you want to tell it as a story.'

"I didn't really like it, however I decided to go with Scott's plan, mostly because I knew the new team was led by a Driver. We put the current situation first but gave the notebook a covering note to point out that 'my' story, the chronological detail, was included in a clearly marked section. The new team was pleased and the team leader thought it was great."

upcoming chapters. You will find that you fit best in one of those four styles of communication. Perhaps one out of every four of your customers will be of the same Social Style as you. In those cases the same behaviors might make you both comfortable. In three out of four cases, however, the things that might help you feel comfortable are not likely to have the same effect for the customer.

Success in sales is *not* concerned with making yourself comfortable.

Versatility doesn't mean feeling comfortable in every sales situation. To the contrary, being versatile and successful in sales means at times you purposefully take on a degree of discomfort for yourself, in order to meet your customer's needs.

And this is a reality that may never change. No matter how well you master *Versatile Selling,* there will probably always be sales situations that challenge you to adjust your own comfort zone.

Why is comfort so important? It's a prerequisite to other aspects of the sales process. Without it, customers will not disclose as much information about their needs to you. They will be looking for the "catch" in your recommendation, not focusing on how the solution solves their problems. They will not be as open about their resistance to your suggestion. Trust and comfort are not "nice to have" atmospheric extras. In sales, it's not a question of getting buyers to like you. Rather, it's about creating the relationship that allows a good sales process to move forward.

TENSION

Although there's a tendency to think of all tension as a source of negative stress, that's not really the case. It's more helpful in managing a sales process to think of tension as productive or unproductive.

There are two kinds of tension in every sales situation – *task tension* and *relationship tension.* Relationship tension doesn't serve much positive purpose, but task tension can keep everybody moving toward solutions . . . and sales.

Task tension

Your customer has something to accomplish. Whether it's to plan a family holiday itinerary or to install a new management information system for a 3,000-person organization, there are deadlines to meet and financial implications to take into account. There are specific goals and objectives tied to the potential purchase. There are reputations and personal pride at stake. People are counting on your customer to make good decisions. These and many other forces create a sense of urgency for your client to be smart, be thrifty, be thorough . . . to make the right purchase. That's task tension.

Relationship tension

Relationship tension is just as natural a part of the sales process, but it results much more from the personal connection – or lack of it – between buyer and seller.

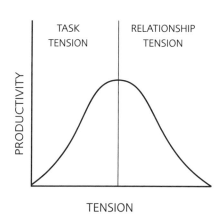

Task and Relationship Tension and Productivity

A certain amount of task tension is good. It increases productivity directed toward the goal you and your customer are accomplishing together. Relationship tension prevents your customer from focusing on task tension. When relationship tension is high, your customer feels uncomfortable and task-directed productivity drops.

At the outset of a sale, your customer may not feel a high level of trust. That lack of trust doesn't mean the customer has a low opinion of you; more likely it's just a matter of the customer not knowing enough about you. That uncertainty about who you are and what you're after creates relationship tension. But relationship tension is not only present at the beginning of the sales process. It can resurface at any point if you are not aware of the dynamics of the interaction. As you begin to uncover needs, customers might feel an increase in relationship tension if it's not perfectly clear you fully understand their unique problems and expectations. Relationship tension also can increase when you reach the point of influencing a final buying decision, and again after the buying decision when concerns often mount about implementation and resolution of the problems the purchase is targeted to solve.

Rising and falling tension

Early in the sales process, task tension may be relatively low. Deadlines may be quite far off. The details of what must be accomplished may be just beginning to become clear. The attention from others who may have future significant roles to play related to the product or service you're selling may not yet be fully engaged in the project.

Relationship tension is unproductive because it suppresses task tension. Task tension, however, can be extremely productive because it is an expression of the customer's sense of urgency and willingness to

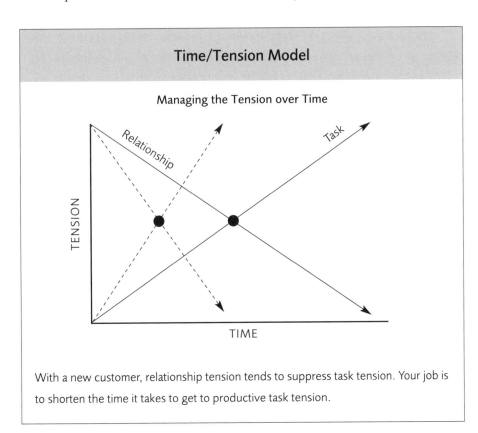

Time/Tension Model

Managing the Tension over Time

Relationship

Task

TENSION

TIME

With a new customer, relationship tension tends to suppress task tension. Your job is to shorten the time it takes to get to productive task tension.

get down to the task at hand. It can work in your favor.

Keeping in mind that success in sales depends upon making customers comfortable, your challenge is to move your customer away from relationship tension as fast as possible so you can focus together on raising the task tension. You and the customer both have things to get done. You don't want your relationship to detract from those tasks.

Even after the initial relationship tension is lessened, you must constantly watch out for an increase in relationship tension – those moments when customers feel angry or frustrated, or suddenly go quiet, even perhaps avoiding your calls. These fight or flight responses require special handling.

In the upcoming chapters on selling to specific Social Styles you'll learn more about this fight or flight concept. You will gain skills to *neutralize* customers who are ready to battle you on all fronts and to *intervene* when it looks as if they are ready to flee or withdraw.

ASSERTIVENESS AND RESPONSIVENESS – THE PRIMARY DIMENSIONS OF INTERACTION

The purpose of *Versatile Selling* is to help you understand what makes different people comfortable, what creates and reduces relationship tension, and how you can modify your behavior to accommodate those differences and make productive task tension work for you.

It is critically important to understand that *Versatile Selling* is not aimed at changing who you are. It doesn't in any way encourage or endorse deception, dishonesty, compromising your integrity or changing what you feel or think. Instead, it aims to help you recognize that people do interact

Behavior and Feeling Defined

Behavior: An observable, measurable, externalized action; something you say or do.

Feeling: An internalized emotion that is not directly evident to observers; something you may or may not disclose through behavior.

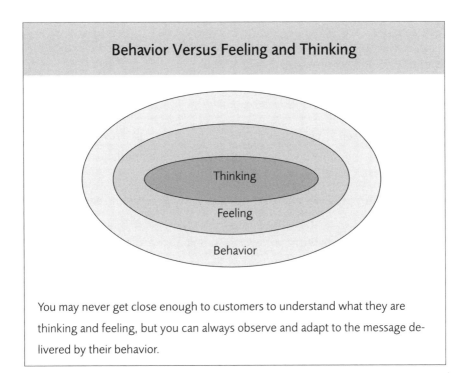

Behavior Versus Feeling and Thinking

Thinking

Feeling

Behavior

You may never get close enough to customers to understand what they are thinking and feeling, but you can always observe and adapt to the message delivered by their behavior.

differently. It teaches you to adapt what you do to sell and serve your customers in the ways they want to be treated, so you sell more effectively. In the end, that serves you and your customers best.

Social scientists have used all kinds of words and phrases to define, classify, measure and describe the kind of behavior we've been discussing. At Wilson Learning, we have focused on the two dimensions that, research has shown, account for the major differences among people. They are therefore the major potential sources of relationship tension. We call these two dimensions assertiveness and responsiveness. We'll take a look at each of them now.

Assertiveness – the key to influencing others

Assertiveness is the way in which a person is perceived as attempting to influence the thoughts and actions of others.

Everybody is assertive. We all spend a lot of time and energy trying to get what we want, but we do it differently. If you view assertiveness

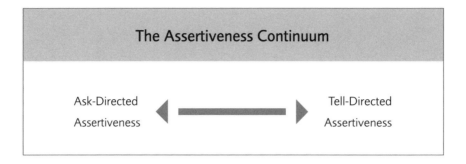

on a continuum, the left end of the scale is *ask-directed* and the right end is *tell-directed.*

People on the ask-directed end of the scale tend to be more subtle and indirect in the way they try to influence others. They ask more questions, tend to suggest or offer ideas, not state decisions. The non-verbal cues you'll get from ask-directed people will also be subtler. They lean back in their chairs when they speak. They'll talk more slowly, allow pauses and appear calm and composed.

People on the tell-directed end of the scale tend to be more up front and demonstrative. They typically speak at a faster pace and often take quick initiative to keep conversations and plans moving. The nonverbal cues from the tell-directed people also are usually more direct. You'll see them leaning forward during the conversation, and everything will sound a bit louder and faster.

Assertiveness Behaviors

Ask-Directed	Tell-Directed
Speaks deliberately, often pausing	Speaks quickly and often firmly
Seldom interrupts others	Often interrupts others
Seldom uses voice for emphasis	Often uses voice for emphasis
Makes many conditional statements	Makes many declarative statements
Tends to lean back	Tends to lean forward

Research shows there is no "best place" on this continuum of assertiveness. As you think about where you fall on this scale, don't worry about being "right." There's no data that demonstrates those who ask more or tell more have a distinctive advantage in influencing others. The research does show, however, that depending on the situation, some assertiveness will be more effective than other behaviors. Your opportunity lies in modifying your own behavior along the assertiveness continuum so that you are influencing in the way that is most comfortable and acceptable to your customer.

Responsiveness – the key to expressing feelings

Responsiveness is the way in which a person is perceived as expressing feelings when relating to others.

There are also two ends to the continuum on responsiveness, which is the scale on which we measure how much expressing our feelings counts for us, when dealing with other people. Because this characteristic is independent of assertiveness we think of the model as flowing top to bottom. Task-directed is at the top of the continuum. People-directed is at the bottom.

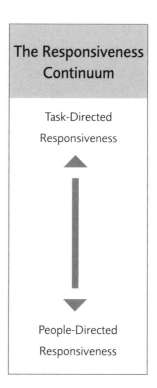

People who are task-directed are usually more reserved in expressing their emotions. Their preference in most situations is to focus first on the task at hand rather than sharing their personal feelings or talking about their personal issues. Only after work issues have been dealt with will they take up interpersonal topics. They will tend to talk more about the facts of the project than about the people involved with it. And they will give nonverbal clues like a composed posture, level tone of

Responsiveness Behaviors	
Task-Directed	**People-Directed**
Talks more about tasks and facts	Talks more about people and relationships
Uses minimal body gestures	Uses broad, expansive body gestures
Shows a narrow range of personal feelings to others	Shows a broad range of personal feelings to others
Uses limited facial expressions	Uses varied and open facial expressions

voice, contained gestures and limited facial expressions.

Those on the other end of this continuum – the people-directed side – generally express their emotions openly and freely. They are inclined to focus on the feelings and relationship issues tied into the task at hand, often believing that task issues are easier to deal with after you have established a personal relationship. They talk frequently about the people on the project team, their working relationships, and building cooperation. Nonverbally, those who are people-directed use broad and varied gestures, a variable tone of voice and more facial expressions. People who are task-directed and people-directed all experience the full range of human feelings; they just express themselves differently in relation to tasks and the people.

Again, it's very important not to attach any judgment of character or effectiveness to these descriptors. There is no right or wrong responsiveness type, no right or wrong assertiveness type. There is no better or worse, just different. We all know people on both ends of the continuum who are effective and successful in their work.

The basis for the Social Style matrix

If you combine the assertiveness and responsiveness continua so they cross at a midpoint, they create a matrix that we call the Social Style matrix. You will find much more detail on the matrix as you read the upcoming chapters.

People who are more tell-directed fall to the right of the midpoint on the matrix; those who are ask-directed fall to the left. People who are task-directed usually land above the midpoint, while those who are people-directed fall below the midpoint. The crossed lines create the four quadrants of Social Styles. In the Social Style matrix:

- People who fall in the upper-left quadrant (ask-directed, task-directed) are identified as *Analyticals*.
- People in the upper-right quadrant (tell-directed, task-directed) are *Drivers*.
- People in the lower-left quadrant (ask-directed, people-directed) are *Amiables*.
- People in the lower-right quadrant (tell-directed, people-directed) are *Expressives*.

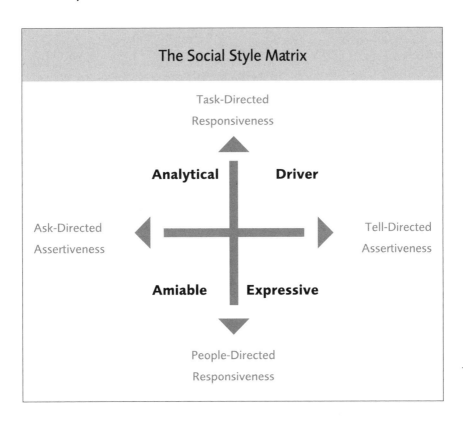

REACTING VERSUS ADAPTING

Habit is a friend – when it comes to getting dressed in the morning or completing any of the hundreds of routine tasks we have to get through in a normal day. It just makes life easier not to have to spend a lot of time in deep reflection about how to brush your teeth. But habit can be a seductive and counterproductive crutch when it comes to selling. Then habit can become a trap.

Three basic steps occur in most human interactions, including a sales encounter:

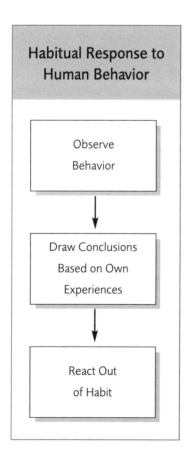

- We observe.
- We draw conclusions about what we see.
- We respond to what we observe and then we observe the outcome of that response.

Habit becomes problematic in sales when our conclusions are based on the assumption that the customer is standing in *our* shoes. When we limit our understanding to projecting only from our own thoughts, experiences and feelings about similar situations, we may misinterpret what the customer thinks and feels.

Unfortunately this practice is very common. Too often our actions are simply instinctive reactions based on what we know will make *us* comfortable. It's a bit of self-preservation, which usually results in doing for a new customer what we've always done for just about every other customer. We rely on just one set of predictable patterns of behavior because that lets us stay in our own comfort zone. As we noted before, three times out of four or more, this won't be your customer's comfort zone – nor your customer's buying zone.

A more productive pattern is to focus on being versatile instead of habitual:

- Identify the customer's Social Style, taking into account what you will learn about Social Styles in this book.
- Reflect on the customer's style, thinking about what makes customers of this Social Style feel comfortable.
- Modify your own behaviors in ways that will create customer comfort.

The payoff? Research shows a strong correlation between high Versatility – adapting instead of reacting – and high performance in sales. You can improve your Versatility immediately with only small adaptations, but for really significant results, you should practice the skills we will describe in this book at every opportunity.

Versatile Response to Human Behavior

Identify
Identify the customer's
Social Style.
"She/he is. . . . "

Reflect
Based on the customer's Social
Style, reflect on and describe
the customer's expectations for
comfort during the sales
process.
"So she/he needs. . . . "

Modify
Decide how to Modify your behaviors to maximize the potential for sales effectiveness
throughout the interaction.
"Therefore I will. . . . "

RELATING, DISCOVERING, ADVOCATING AND SUPPORTING

Versatile Selling is not a sales process, nor does it only "work" inside a particular sales process. In fact, the lessons we hope to impart and the insights you'll gain learning about Social Styles and Versatility can be applied to any sales system or process you may use.

Nonetheless, about a million people around the world have found Wilson Learning's Counselor approach a very effective sales process, and *Versatile Selling* fits by design with that approach. For nearly forty years, Wilson Learning has been teaching and refining its pioneering Counselor selling approach to salespeople around the world and in all business sectors.

Although *Versatile Selling* will not provide extensive instruction in this four-step sales approach, we will recommend behaviors you can use in all four stages to best accommodate customers of different Social Styles.

Therefore it's important to have a basic understanding of these four key terms – Relating, Discovering, Advocating and Supporting – so you'll be able to best apply *Versatile Selling* to whatever system you use.*

Relating

Relating means building trust and creating a sense of credibility. If a customer doesn't feel it, you really don't have the customer. It is in this stage of the sales process when you should be focused on reducing or eliminating relationship tension.

As you recall, high relationship tension depresses task tension and productivity drops as a result.

As we cover the role Relating plays in selling to customers in each of the different Social Styles we'll be talking to you about:

---

*For a complete description of the Counselor approach, see *Win-Win Selling: The Original 4-Step Counselor Approach for Building Long-Term Relationships with Customers* (Nova Vista Publishing, 2003), another title in the Wilson Learning Library.

- *Propriety* – meeting buyers' expectations about appropriate business customs and behaviors, everything from dress to the use of jargon.
- *Competence* – exhibiting the ability and background to help buyers solve their problems.
- *Commonality* – finding areas of mutual interest, values or experience with buyers.
- *Intent* – making clear that your motives are to work in the best interest of your customers.

One of the most important Relating tools in Wilson Learning's Counselor selling approach is the use of Purpose, Process and Payoff statements when first meeting with a customer and at the start of discussions and documents. In the Social Styles chapters we'll include recommendations about how the content and delivery style of these statements should vary for each style and depend upon where you are in the sales process – Relating, Discovering, Advocating or Supporting. The basics of these statements, however, will remain the same:

- *Purpose.* One of the first things you want to do is remind a customer why you are meeting. The Purpose statement lets the buyer know the specific reason you are together and what you hope to accomplish during the sales call. For example, you might say, "My purpose today is to share some information about myself, my company, and the products and services we offer. I also want to find out more about your company and the needs you have that led you to invite me to come talk to you. Does that sound like a productive plan to you?"
- *Process.* You use the process statement to tell buyers what you are going to do and how. For example, "I'd like to begin by discussing some questions I think you might have about me and my company, and then spend some time to make sure I understand in a bit more detail the problems you're dealing with and the needs you have for getting them resolved."

- *Payoff.* Payoff statements tell your customers the benefits you'll both get from the time spent together. "You'll learn something about us. We'll learn something about you. And together we can determine whether our company is a potential resource for meeting your needs."

Discovering

During this stage in the sales process your challenge is to establish and clarify your customer's needs. You objective is to develop a mutual understanding of the customer's situation and establish where there is an urgent need for help and attention. What is the problem for which you have a solution?

Discovering requires effective questioning and listening skills that help clarify a customer's buying motives and buying conditions. Counselor-selling-style questions fall into several useful categories:

- *Permission Questions.* "We offer a variety of solutions that might fit your needs. Is it okay if I ask you a few questions first to make sure we talk about the possibilities that are best-suited for your situation?"
- *Fact-Finding Questions.* You're after facts and data and will probably get a lot of short answers. "What kind of equipment are you using now? How many units does it produce in a day? How often does it require maintenance?"
- *Feeling-Finding Questions.* These will help you understand a buyer's opinions, feelings, values, and beliefs – and they are especially powerful when used in combination with fact-finding questions. "How do you feel about the overall reliability and effectiveness of the equipment you're using now? In your opinion, is your current daily production rate as good as it needs to be for your long-term success?"
- *Best-Least Questions.* "What do you like best about the fringe benefits you provide employees? What do you like least?"

- *Magic-Wand Questions.* Get your customer dreaming a little. "If you could wave a magic wand and make this problem go away, what would your business look like?"
- *Tell-Me-More Questions.* When you need more detail, ask, "Can you tell me a bit more about that? Could you elaborate a little?"
- *Catch-All Questions.* "Is there anything else that I should know about your current equipment or situation? Is there anything else you'd like to accomplish with this upgrade? Is there anything I forgot to ask you?"

Three techniques that contribute to effective listening during the Discovering stage are:

- *Responsive Listening,* which includes using verbal and nonverbal behavior and signals to reinforce what your customer is saying and to make it clear you are listening attentively.
- *Restatement,* which is a process for paraphrasing what the buyer says in order to summarize what you hear and to verify that you have understood correctly. "In other words, you're saying. . . . "
- *Checking,* which is a method similar to *Restatement* but focused on making sure you have an accurate understanding of the customer's situation. "Did you say you have 2.65 million items in inventory?"

Advocating

It is during the Advocating stage of the sales process that you focus on influencing the buyer's decision-making. This is when you establish that there is a need for what you have to offer and that what you have to offer will do the job.

One of the key points here is that you need to truly believe in your own products and services. But also, it's tough to close a sale if you don't also develop your customer into an advocate for your solutions. That can happen naturally if your customer trusts you – thanks to your Relating – and you clearly understand the needs – because of what you accomplish while Discovering. Those two steps are critical to putting you in position to make the sale, but Advocating skills are essential to finishing the job. Regardless of how comfortable prospects feel with you or how sure you are that you understand their unique buying needs, you won't make a sale if *they* don't see a compelling need for your product or service.

The upcoming chapters on selling to specific Social Styles will provide Advocating ideas that will help you find the shortest, straightest and most persuasive path to helping your customers believe in and buy your products or services.

Supporting

There are four pillars of the Supporting stage in a sales process:

1. *Supporting the Buying Decision*. This can begin before an actual contract is signed if a customer begins to feel some buyer's remorse or last-minute uncertainty about the deal. It is also important after the check is written, however. Your purpose is to keep the customer feeling good about the purchase.

2. *Managing the Implementation*. After the sale you may hand off your customer to others in your organization to handle the implementation. This can be a nervous time for the customer so it's important to orchestrate a seamless transition that's designed to assure satisfaction.

3. *Dealing with Dissatisfaction*. Things can go wrong after the sale, often as a result of something totally outside your control, perhaps even as a result of some misuse or abuse by the client company. Don't look for blame, look for resolution. Even though the "sale" may be done you can't really bow out of relationships with the customers. In fact, you are the first person dissatisfied customers will turn to when something goes wrong.

4. *Enhancing the Relationship*. It's almost always easier to earn new business from an existing satisfied customer than it is to sell to new customers. When things go well with one sale it provides a great

opportunity for exploring what else you might be able to provide for the customer's company.

BACK-UP BEHAVIOR – FIGHT OR FLIGHT

When tension in sales relationships reaches the point where customers start saying, "I can't take it anymore," they begin exhibiting Back-Up Behavior. You are now at the moment when Versatility is needed most urgently. Your customer has reached the point of "fight or flight," and the way you respond will determine whether you will lose the sale opportunity or survive to get to the next step.

As described earlier in this chapter, tension exists on two levels in all sales relationships – in the relationship between buyer and seller, and in the task to be accomplished. Both kinds of tension play an important role in connecting in a win-win sales scenario. Task tension provides a certain sense of urgency about what must get done to reach a goal – for the customer to make a wise purchase and the salesperson to close a solid deal. Relationship tension, on the other hand, suppresses the development of task tension and thus can inhibit you and your customer's progress through the sales cycle.

When interpersonal tension becomes extreme, however, relationships begin to unravel and productivity drops off, as you'll see in the chart to the right.

When they feel increasing

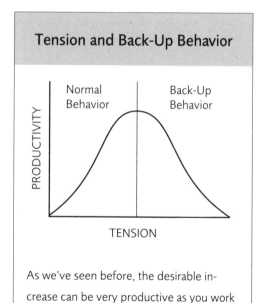

Tension and Back-Up Behavior

Normal Behavior

Back-Up Behavior

PRODUCTIVITY

TENSION

As we've seen before, the desirable increase can be very productive as you work with customers. If relationship tension becomes too strong, however, Back-Up Behavior begins and productivity decreases.

The Bad News about Back-Up Behavior

By the time your customers start exhibiting Back-Up Behavior you are in pretty deep trouble. They are looking for a way out, either through "fight or flight."

The human race has come a long way in finding ways to react to stress, but we're all still tied biophysically to the primitive instinctual responses of fight or flight when faced with threatening situations. A dangerous situation unfolds, there's a rush of adrenaline, and we make an instantaneous decision about what we're going to do to protect ourselves. A 21st century salesperson pushing too hard to close a deal doesn't really present the same sense of stress as a saber-toothed tiger looking for lunch in a loincloth, but the basic responses are the same: Turn and run or stand and fight.

People's Social Styles provide useful clues about what Back-Up Behaviors to expect. But fight or flight behaviors are not always revealed in obvious ways.

Amiables and Analyticals are ask-directed on the responsiveness dimension. Their tendency in Back-Up mode is toward flight. Despite any anger or deep frustration they might feel, however, you won't see any shouting or table pounding as they walk away. They will probably be much more subtle, and quietly withdraw. An Amiable tends to acquiesce, giving in rather than fighting on principle ("Sure, do whatever you want."). An Analytical will withdraw through avoidance, not returning calls, putting a low priority on the task or relationship ("Sorry, haven't had time to run through the details. Call me later."). They are fleeing from the task or relationship.

Expressives and Drivers, who are tell-directed on the responsiveness dimension and more inclined to fight when in Back-Up, tend to stand their ground based on principles or positions. A Driver will leave nothing uncertain ("Okay, let me tell you what you're going to do to fix this: First, you will. . . . "). An Expressive will make a point with typical emotional overtones ("I can't believe you're doing this to me! I'm holding you personally responsible.").

Back-Up Behavior is strictly defensive. It's all aimed at self-protection, which makes it virtually impossible to achieve your sales objectives – or for your customers to find solutions for their needs or negociate well. To salvage any chance of getting back on task, you've got to lead a customer to a more productive state of mind.

relationship tension, most people tend to retreat deeper and deeper into their behavioral comfort zones. They begin to exhibit inflexible, less versatile versions of the behaviors normally associated with their Social Styles. As you might expect, people with the same Social Style tend to continue to behave in similar, predictable patterns when tension gets too high for comfort.

Initial Flight and Fight Responses to Tension

Analytical | Driver

FLIGHT | FIGHT

Amiable | Expressive

You can see in the chart on the right that the first sign that ask-directed Analyticals and Amiables give of their discomfort is a tendency to *flight* – which may not mean actually running away, but rather, avoiding you, not returning calls, not having time for you, etc. The tell-directed Drivers and Expressives tend at first to *fight* – challenging, bullying, and so on, if the pressure gets too intense.

The subject of Back-Up Behaviors demonstrated by people of various Social Styles is quite complex, more so than we can cover in this book. If you keep yourself alert to signs of the first stage of fight or flight behavior of your customer's own style and respond correctly, you can head off trouble.*

The good news about Back-Up Behavior is that customer relationships that have reached a tenuous point can be saved, even when tension levels leave you on the brink of disaster. Tools for managing conflict with customers and the specific nuances needed for each style will be discussed later in each chapter about the four Social Styles.

---

*For more detail and in-depth discussion about Back-Up Behavior and how to handle it, see *The Social Styles Handbook* (Nova Vista Publishing, 2004), another title in the Wilson Learning Library.

Back-Up Behaviors

ANALYTICAL – AVOIDING

- Avoids confrontation
- Draws attention away from an issue
- Retreats to other distractions
- Delays decisions

DRIVER – AUTOCRATIC

- Confronts others
- Focuses on the issue
- Looks for rationale
- Becomes demanding

AMIABLE – ACQUIESCING

- Smooths relationships
- Yields to others' viewpoints
- Wavers on opinion; hesitates
- Gives in; withdraws support

EXPRESSIVE – ATTACKING

- Confronts others
- Verbalizes judgmental feelings
- Blames others personally
- Shows extreme emotion

We'll discuss Back-Up Behaviors – and how to handle them – for each Social Style in Chapters 4 through 7. But first, let's explore a very useful process. You can use it when working with customers of all Social Styles whenever you perceive that relationship tension and conflict are rising and you see the start of Back-Up Behavior. It's called the LSCPA Model. Since the applications of LSCPA really vary only slightly (but significantly) as you work with customers of different Social Styles, you may want to bookmark this section. That way you can refer to it in the context of the specific Social Styles we'll focus on later.

THE LSCPA MODEL FOR HANDLING BACK-UP BEHAVIOR

One proven way to deal with Back-Up Behavior with all Social Styles is by using the LSCAP model: **L**isten, **S**hare, **C**larify, **P**roblem-Solve, **A**sk for **A**ction. It's an effective approach for dealing with conflict in business and personal situations that is recommended by sales experts and mental health professionals.

Listen

It is important to hear a customer's concerns completely. Pay attention for the facts, the beliefs and the feelings that are expressed. Encourage your customers to talk openly about anything that is troubling them, and listen until there is nothing more to hear. Pay attention to body language as you listen, and even after you listen. Look for clues in your customers' eyes and movements that will reveal their comfort or tension levels.

The true power of this kind of listening is your acknowledgment of the customers' concerns. Most likely, at this stage they are not interested in hearing rational explanations for what has gone wrong; they just want to know you hear what's bothering them. You are listening out of respect, not so you can dispute the facts of the situation.

Don't interrupt. Stay calm. Use your own body language to demonstrate that you are attentive and encourage customers to keep talking.

Share

Your goal in this stage is to make it clear to customers you understand what they are saying and feeling. You may not agree with what you are hearing, but that doesn't matter. You need to share your customers concerns and understand their perceptions of the situation without judging, or worse, debating them. The goal is to help ease customers back to a state of calm; challenging them at this point is not a good way to soothe frayed emotions.

Show your empathy. Use phrases such as, "You're angry and I can understand why," and "You seem to feel strongly about that." Avoid arguing at all costs.

Clarify

In many cases, the concerns your customers first raise will not be the real sources of their frustration. Listen and then restate what you hear to encourage your customers to help you fully understand what is happening. Ask questions to make sure you are truly identifying the root causes of their problems. For example, a customer may show anger with you about something that actually begins within his or her own organization. You may be surprised by a strong negative reaction that seems clearly related to pricing, for example, even though cost did not seem to be an issue as your negotiations progressed. Is expense truly the issue, or has an internal policy change within your customer's organization created new purchase barriers? You must find out.

- Restate your customers' problems in your own words and ask questions to verify you've understood the problem from your customer's point of view.
- Turn objections into questions. For example: "You say the delivery date we agreed on won't work. Why exactly is that? Has something changed since we first discussed this timeframe?"
- Ask as many questions as you need answered to understand all the facts and all the feelings at play in this stage of Back-Up.

Some customers may not understand what their problems are, or may not want to blame their own companies. This kind of questioning can help you and them pinpoint the challenge and difficulties.

Problem-Solve

Once you fully understand the problems, start thinking and talking again about new solutions. Assure your customers you have dealt with similar situations before and can handle theirs, too. Then, put together a strategy that addresses the true concerns in a timely, satisfactory way.

This takes you back into the Discovering stage of your sales process, described earlier in this chapter. Be certain you clearly understand your customers' objections, frustrations, or fears, and then offer solutions that will solve their problems and dispel concerns.

Ask for Action

The final step in LSCPA is to get feedback about what you propose to your customers in response to their dissatisfaction and then to ask for action. Ask if the concern has been addressed adequately. Agree on a solution. Make plans to follow through on what you have agreed upon for next steps.

Although LSCPA is laid out in what seems to be a logical, step-by-step sequence, the reality is you may have to cycle through some of the steps several times before you are able to restore a customer's comfort. It might also seem reasonable to expect you can accomplish all of these recovery goals in one meeting, but depending upon the complexity of the situation and the number of people involved in the purchase, it could take much longer.

ADAPTING LSCPA TO FIGHT OR FLIGHT BEHAVIOR

It is important that you also adapt LSCPA based upon your customer's fight or flight tendencies. The adaptation occurs primarily in the *Listen* and *Share* steps. For fight behaviors, the strategy is to *neutralize*. For flight behaviors, the strategy is to *intervene*.

To help *neutralize* your tell-directed Driver and Expressive customers in Back-Up, who are most inclined to be in the *fight* mode:

If you are dealing with a *Fight* Style of Back-Up, such as *Attacking* or *Autocrative* behaviors, then you can use the *neutralize* strategy. This means letting the customer vent by using the following techniques.

- Allow them to get out their feelings in order to get past their defensive fighting stance so you can identify the real problems that may be behind their anger.

- Accept their comments without judgment or automatic rebuttal.
- Listen to their upset feelings, with your goal being to demonstrate you accept their differences with you and value their business.
- Don't interrupt and don't correct.
- Ask enough questions to get the venting started and finished.
- Stay attentive, relaxed, and non-confrontational.
- Once the issues are completely aired, *clarify* the core problem before moving back to problem-solving. This is the **C** step in LSCPA.

If you are dealing with a *Flight* style of Back-Up, such as *Avoiding* or *Acquiescing* behaviors, then you adapt LSCPA with an *intervene* strategy. This means you draw feelings out, using the following techniques:

- Your first challenge is to draw out information and feelings. Get the issue on the table so it can be addressed rather than ignored.
- Ask question to find out what is bothering them.
- Be persistent, but not pushy.
- Try to uncover the specifics of what has gone wrong. This may be difficult at first. Ask-directed customers in flight often prefer to be vague and evasive.
- Show genuine concern.
- Acknowledge and confirm their feelings. Assure them it is okay to disagree with you.
- Share your own feelings about the situation. This can help encourage more open disclosure of concerns on their parts.
- Once the issues are completely aired, *clarify* the core problem before moving back to the task of problem-solving. This is the **C** step in LSCPA.

SUMMARY
Versatile Selling, as you move forward, will refer regularly to the foundational language you've found in this chapter. Remember these ba-

sics and you'll be well prepared for the specific *Versatile Selling* ideas that come next:

- Success in sales is directly tied to customer comfort, not necessarily your own.
- Creating comfort requires Versatility.
- Tension can focus on the relationship and on the task at hand. The goal is to manage tension to make it productive, reducing relationship tension and allowing task tension to rise, so that the search for a good solution can proceed.
- Versatility means adapting your behavior to meet the concerns and expectations of your customers, which will vary according to Social Style – and which at times may mean you have to make yourself somewhat uncomfortable.
- Your customers' comfort zones and typical behaviors fall into one of the four Social Styles.
- Styles are defined by two key dimensions: assertiveness (which is related to influencing others) and responsiveness (which is related to expressing feelings).
- The four styles are Analytical, Driver, Amiable and Expressive.
- The key stages of a sales process are Relating, Discovering, Advocating and Supporting.
- The **L**isten – **S**hare – **C**larify – **P**roblem **S**olve – **A**sk for **A**ction process, called LSCPA, is a powerful tool for handling conflict in business and personal situations. It has special modifications for helping to resolve conflict depending on the style of the customer.
- Back-Up Behavior, the natural response to higher tension than the customer feels comfortable with, involves *fight* for Drivers and Expressives, and *flight* for Analyticals and Amiables. We'll say more in detail in each of the upcoming chapters dedicated to each style.

3 | Social Styles

Living is easy with eyes closed,
misunderstanding all you see. . . .
JOHN LENNON AND PAUL MCCARTNEY

Perception is reality. What we see is what we believe. Unfortunately what we see isn't always true, especially when watching customers for cues to help us sell to them – not because we're misled, but more likely because we don't read the signs very well. Learning and using the Social Style matrix can open your eyes to new ways of seeing things, help reduce relationship tension, and make you a more successful salesperson. You'll both make more sales and be a better problem-solver for each customer you work with.

You can never know for sure what your customers are thinking – or feeling. But watch and listen closely; you *can* see and hear what they're doing and saying. With practice using Social Styles, you will increase your awareness, improve your powers of observation, and sharpen your ability to draw accurate conclusions about the significance of your customers' behaviors. Their actions are telling and showing you what it will take to earn their trust and confidence. Their buying behaviors are part of a broader, predictable lifelong pattern. Your customers' behaviors provide useful and reliable clues about how you can adapt your own behavior to make them most comfortable, and most likely to buy from you.

FOUR KINDS OF CUSTOMERS

Nearly 40 years of research by Wilson Learning, with more than two *million* people around the world, show we can quite accurately group people into four general Social Styles: Analyticals, Drivers, Expressives and Amiables. The daily application of knowledge and skills by people trained in Social Styles also shows that understanding the implications of these styles can help us understand each other better. We can learn to "read" and respond to people in ways that expand rather than restrict our appreciation for each other's differences. That's why you often hear people who have taken the Wilson Learning Social Styles training say that it is a life-changing experience.

You might be wondering how generalizing about people's behavior can lead to an enriched understanding of them – and of course, ourselves. After all, generalizing is often associated with narrow-mindedness. Using Social Styles requires you to make generalizations, but with the intent of helping you deepen, not flatten, your understanding of different people's behavior.

We all are creatures of habit. Habits are useful because they allow us to do repetitive tasks without thinking about what we're doing. They define our comfort zone. But habitual thinking, and making judgments, can interfere when we are trying to expand our ability to perceive and learn new things. Habits are hard to change, too, so it's no surprise that when we need to learn to look at or do something differently, we run up against the wall of established habit.

Judgments are conclusions we draw about another person. They can be positive or negative, but in either case they lead easily to stereotyping and misunderstanding about individual differences.

The way out of the trap of habit and judgment is to focus only on observable behavior. This is the realm of Social Styles. While this may appear to be judgment and generalization, it differs from these in two crucial ways. First, behavior is tied to what is on the "outside" of the person (words, tone, and body language), not what's on the "inside" (thoughts, feelings, character or personality). Second, the conclusions we draw from Social Style concepts are research-based, independent of habitual or subjective opinion. You don't often have a database of two million people to back your thinking!

FINDING AND MINDING YOUR OWN SOCIAL STYLE

Where do you fit in the Social Styles matrix?

There's little doubt that one of your first impulses as you learn about the four Social Styles will be to do some self-analysis. Follow that curiosity; it's a healthy sign you are on track to grasp one of the core concepts in *Versatile Selling.* You are open to seeing yourself in new ways.

Identifying styles is a two-part process. First, you need to know yourself. Second, you must understand how your natural style compares, complements or differs from your customers. Your ultimate goal, of course, is to be able to use that knowledge to strategically adapt your behaviors to create a more comfortable relationship with your buyers and increase sales.

It is important to remember when identifying styles, however, that Social Style is *not* about intelligence, personality, character, aptitude, performance or correctness.

A Social Style *is* observable behavior. It's what you see and hear when you watch others. Gestures. Body position. Tone of voice. Facial expressions and responses in reaction to your questions and comments. A focus on the facts or feelings of an issue or situation. And Social Style is what *others* see when they watch you. That can be the tricky part of putting yourself into the matrix. Why? Because about 70 percent of the time the way we perceive ourselves is different from the way others see us.

As a result, it may be much easier for you to objectively and accurately determine the Social Styles of others than it is for yourself. That's okay. When it comes to communicating, it is less important where we see ourselves in the Social Styles matrix than how we perceive others, and it's also less important than knowing how customers perceive us.

As you try to determine your own style, try to step outside of yourself. Objectively ask, "If I were seeing this behavior in someone else, and I didn't know the thoughts or feelings behind it, what would I think?" In fact, as you first try to determine your own style, share this information with others and see if they agree. The Social Styles profiler at the end of this chapter will help you practice what you'll learn in the coming pages.

The most important thing is to be clear about what your customers need and expect. You can't change your own Social Style. We are not suggesting that you move to another quadrant – to be someone other than yourself. You really don't and can't move very far out of your comfort zone. To try to "be" another Social Style will be perceived as manipulative and insincere. You therefore can only work within your own style, and learn to make rather small modifications and adjustments to your own behaviors. Moving to another quadrant is what most people are afraid they are being asked to do – but that is not what Social Styles is all about.

UNDERSTANDING THE POWER OF SOCIAL STYLES

As we've seen in Chapter 2, there are four main clusters of consistent behavior represented by the four quadrants of the Social Styles matrix – called Analyticals, Drivers, Amiables and Expressives. The matrix is created by categorizing behavior on two different dimensions.

The first dimension is *assertiveness* – the way in which we try to influence the thoughts and actions of others. The second dimension is *responsiveness* – the way we express our feelings when relating to others.

No two people who share the same Social Style behave the same way in all situations. But you are far more likely to connect quickly and most easily with customers whose behavior falls in the same quadrant as you. The world population actually divides roughly into equal numbers of Analyticals, Drivers, Amiables and Expressives. So this means you've got a great deal in common with about 25 percent of the population. You are similar to them on both dimensions of behavior –

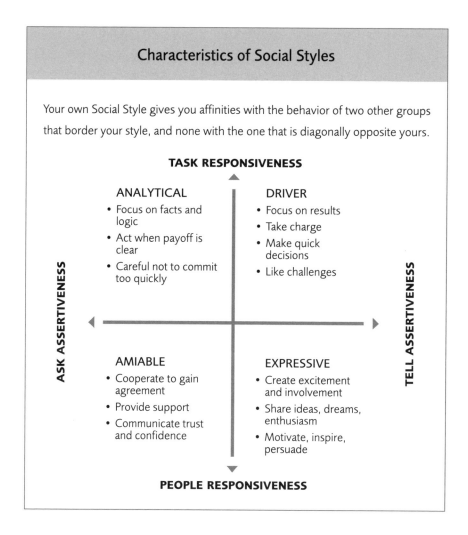

Characteristics of Social Styles

Your own Social Style gives you affinities with the behavior of two other groups that border your style, and none with the one that is diagonally opposite yours.

TASK RESPONSIVENESS

ASK ASSERTIVENESS

TELL ASSERTIVENESS

ANALYTICAL
- Focus on facts and logic
- Act when payoff is clear
- Careful not to commit too quickly

DRIVER
- Focus on results
- Take charge
- Make quick decisions
- Like challenges

AMIABLE
- Cooperate to gain agreement
- Provide support
- Communicate trust and confidence

EXPRESSIVE
- Create excitement and involvement
- Share ideas, dreams, enthusiasm
- Motivate, inspire, persuade

PEOPLE RESPONSIVENESS

assertiveness and responsiveness.

This also means you've got at least something in common with 50 percent of the remaining population. That's because your quadrant in the matrix shares sides with two other styles, which means you are similar in either your assertiveness or your responsiveness to people whose accustomed behavior falls in those adjacent quadrants.

Naturally, that leaves 25 percent of the population with whom you share no similarities in assertive or responsive behaviors. Wherever you land on the matrix, these are the people in the quadrant that is diagonally across from you. No sides of your quadrant touch this group's sides. Your assertive and responsive behaviors are actually diametrically opposed. Not surprisingly, this is the group with whom you may have the greatest difficulty communicating comfortably. The graphic below shows where you share behaviors and where you don't.

Versatile Selling is not a guide to picking a new best friend. You don't necessarily have to like every customer on a personal level. But being versatile and being able to make more customers comfortable does mean learning to bend, even when the style differences make it clear you and your customer respond to the world from opposite points of view. Let's look at the four styles in general now.

Shared Behavior Among Social Style Groups

Social Style	Share Assertiveness (Ask vs. Tell) Behavior with:	Share Responsiveness (Task vs. People) Behavior with:	Share No Behavior with:
Analyticals	Amiables	Drivers	Expressives
Drivers	Expressives	Analyticals	Amiables
Amiables	Analyticals	Expressives	Drivers
Expressives	Drivers	Amiables	Analyticals

For your particular Social Style, two other style groups have similarities and one does not. For example, if you are an Expressive, you are tell-directed on the assertiveness dimension and people-directed on the responsiveness dimension. That means you share assertive behavior styles with Drivers because you both are tell-directed. You share responsive behavior styles with Amiables because you are both people-directed. You don't share any styles of behavior with Analyticals – speaking here in terms of your respective natural comfort zones, not your ability to adapt and move towards theirs.

ANALYTICALS

Analyticals typically approach the world asking questions and staying on task. They want to examine as much information as possible before moving ahead with projects, and they typically do so using logical, orderly processes.

People who are Analyticals are often perceived as deliberate, thorough, and inclined to follow procedures. They weigh all the alternatives in any situation and are usually steadfast in doing whatever needs to be done. They tend to be conservative, businesslike and persistent in their relationships. Analyticals are most likely to pursue goals only after they have eliminated as much risk as possible and have compiled plenty of data to support a project's purpose and practicality.

Getting the picture? When you hear people describe Analyticals they often say they:

- Seem technically oriented and often seek structure, certainty and evidence before they make decisions.
- Appear quiet and unassuming and usually don't show much emotion when dealing with others.
- Are not likely to initiate social connections with people they don't know, and are very likely to remain guarded in a new relationship until trust and confidence are built.
- Like to see how far they can keep going with existing ideas and procedures before they're ready to try something new.

Every Social Style has its strengths. Most common among Analyticals:

- They create and find solid solutions because they rely on facts and logic.
- They make thorough use of all available resources, which makes their solutions practical and persuasive.
- They like to discover new ways to solve persistent problems.

The Analytical Style

Verbal and Nonverbal Cues	Reserved. Few gestures. Proper speech. Formal posture and appearance. Listens well. Deliberate rate of speech.
Work Style	Fairly independent. Follows structured approaches.
Attitude about Time	"Take time to deal with matters objectively and logically. Move with deliberation."
Attitude about Accomplishment	"The process used for getting results is almost as important as the results themselves."
Attitude about Others	"Relationships take time to develop, and someone else will probably make the initial effort to make a new contact."
Natural Work Activity Strengths	Planning and organizing.
Personal Motivator	Respect: Seeks to enhance reputation as a technical expert by making the right decision in the right way. Values being recognized for accomplishments and respected for expertise.
Common Misperceptions about Analyticals	No feelings and no ability to have fun.

- They are competent at working out all details of a problem and then getting the job done right.

A common misperception about Analyticals is that they don't have feelings and they don't know how to have fun. Analyticals are systematic thinkers, but we've been in enough raucous workshops with accountants, engineers and others who typically fall into this style to tell you Analyticals are definitely not unfeeling or humorless.

DRIVERS

Drivers like the challenge of getting things done. They take charge, make quick decisions, and keep moving quickly toward results.

Like Analyticals, Drivers are often perceived as businesslike but even more results-oriented and far more likely to take initiative. Drivers like to challenge new ideas and respond quickly to all situations. Just about everything they do will be straightforward, decisive and quick.

You'll notice that Drivers are people who seem most comfortable pursuing goals when they are in charge. These are the folks who have the knack for mapping out directions and having others see them to completion. Drivers are risk takers. They want to make things happen, and view every new problem as just another exciting challenge to handle. In fact, they thrive on challenge.

You'll know you are in the company of Drivers when you hear them being described as people who:

- Are often direct and to the point with others.
- Seem to have strong opinions and convictions.
- Like to initiate, control and run on self-motivation.
- Tend to be efficient, hard working and focused on bottom-line results.

A Driver's strengths often include:

- Confidence, competence and a take-charge attitude.
- A willingness to take on new challenges and a preference for taking on things others often see as difficult to master.
- An ability to direct and productively coordinate the work of others.
- A sense of responsibility for making things happen.

Drivers are independent, action-oriented and want to be in control. That is a powerful and quick combination that can sometimes lead to

The Driver Style	
Verbal and Nonverbal Cues	Serious. Formal posture. Restrained gestures. Rapid speech. Direct. Voice inflection varies little, usually only to emphasize important points.
Work Style	Independent.
Attitude about Time	"Use it efficiently to get desired results."
Attitude about Accomplishment	"Achieve strong results in the shortest time possible."
Attitude about Others	"Relationships are important but secondary until a task is defined and competency to deal with it is established."
Natural Work Activity Strengths	Initiating and monitoring.
Personal Motivator	Power: Seeks to control the tangible resources of a project such as time, budget, people. Prefers to be given options and probabilities and allowed to make own decisions. Values receiving more authority, control or power over the situation or environment.
Common Misperceptions about Drivers	Impersonal and pushy because they focus on tasks and control their emotions.

the misperception that Drivers are impersonal, pushy and hard-hearted. They do have feelings; they just don't always show them.

AMIABLES

Amiables, like Analyticals, are ask-directed, but the questions they bring to their work are often more focused, at least initially, on the people involved in a task than the task itself. Amiables are concerned with

The Amiable Style	
Verbal and Nonverbal Cues	Warm, friendly and open. Relaxed posture. Slow speech. Pleasant and soft voice. Open and eager facial expressions.
Work Style	With others.
Attitude about Time	"Take time to establish relationships and to make steady progress through a slow, sure pace."
Attitude about Accomplishment	"The best results come through people working together."
Attitude about Others	"People are the most important asset in any project and collaborating with others is the best way to get things done."
Natural Work Activity Strengths	Coaching and counseling.
Personal Motivator	Approval: Seeks to promote or gain agreement from others and to be included as part of the group or team. Values receiving others' approval and having a positive impact on others.
Common Misperceptions about Amiables	Places too much emphasis on relationships, move too slowly, and doesn't get results.

cooperating, providing support and reaching agreement.

Amiables are often perceived as the quiet unassuming members in a team or group. They supply a social lubricant to these groups. They are warm, friendly listeners, easy to get along with, and enjoy personal contact and shared responsibility.

The first step in pursuing goals for Amiables often is to establish strong personal ties with others involved in the project.

The traits that describe Amiables include these:

- They accept others easily and place a high value and priority on getting along.
- They like to minimize interpersonal conflict whenever possible.
- They are easy to get to know and easy to work with.
- They appear quiet, cooperative and supportive.

The strengths Amiables bring to the workplace include:

- Giving good advice and counsel.
- Helping where needed, and providing positive comments about the work, contributions and accomplishment of others.
- Communicating high levels of trust and confidence in others.
- Making people feel comfortable about themselves.

Amiables are not inclined to move ahead without strong support from others to back them up, so they are sometimes misperceived as risk-averse and slow decision makers. They want time to build relationships and they prefer plenty of feedback and cooperation before saying yes or no to a step in a project.

EXPRESSIVES

Expressives bring a lot of energy to their work and are eager and effective in sharing their ideas and getting people around them involved to make things happen. They fall on the same side of the assertiveness scale as Drivers. They are tell-directed but more like Amiables than Drivers on the responsiveness scale; Expressives tend to focus more on the people involved in a task than the task itself.

Expressives are perceived as energetic, inspiring and emotional. They are comfortable taking the lead in social situations, and are willing to invest time and energy into conversation before feeling compelled to move on to tackling the task at hand.

Intuition plays a major role in decision-making by Expressives. They tend to act on what "feels right." It doesn't take much to get an

The Expressive Style

Verbal and Nonverbal Cues	Energetic and enthusiastic. Gestures that are open and wide. Voice that is loud and varied. Fast-paced and lively.
Work Style	With others.
Attitude about Time	"Move fast, but spend time energizing others, sharing visions, dreams and ideas."
Attitude about Accomplishment	"Get results through people."
Attitude about Others	"It is very important to work with people to help make their own dreams reality."
Natural Work Activity Strengths	Motivating and reinforcing.
Personal Motivator	Recognition: Seeks to be highly visible and to stand out from the crowd, to be seen as unique and showing leadership. Values recognition for accomplishment, publicity, symbols of accomplishment.
Common Misperceptions about Expressives	Flighty, more inclined to tell a joke than discuss a business issue. Not businesslike or task-oriented.

Expressive excited about sharing ideas and dreams. They love to brainstorm and build on other people's insights.

You'll know you are in the presence of Expressives when phrases such as these come to mind:

- Excitable, talkative and intuitive.
- Likes an audience, a bit of applause and general recognition.
- Risk-taker, competitive and spirited.
- Visionary, creative and inspirational.

As is the case with all Social Styles, Expressives bring many strengths to their work, including:

- An ability to energize and inspire others.
- A willingness and ability to stimulate the creative exchange of ideas.
- Enthusiasm and ambition.
- An ability to stretch people's thinking with their own dreams and far-reaching ideas.

Expressives are often misperceived as being too flighty, spending too much time building relationships and telling stories at the expense of being business-like and task oriented.

STYLES WITHIN STYLES

As we pointed out when introducing the power of Social Styles at the beginning of this chapter, there is a wide variation in how people communicate even within each of the four main styles. In fact, you will find a wide range of styles within each quadrant of the Social Styles matrix.

For example, you might have four customers who are all Amiables. In comparison to each other, however, one may be more tell-directed than the others. Another may be significantly more ask-directed than the other three Amiables. The third might be relatively more task-directed than the others, and the fourth might be extremely more people-directed than any of the others. They are all still Amiables – all considered to be ask-directed on the assertiveness scale and people-directed on the responsive scale.*

The full measure of your Versatility will be taken when you must adapt your sales behaviors to the finer points of distinguishing these kinds of subtleties.

*For more in-depth discussions on this fascinating aspect of Social Styles, see *The Social Styles Handbook* (Nova Vista Publishing, 2004), another title in the Wilson Library.

TIPS AND TOOLS FOR ASSESSING SOCIAL STYLES

We all tend to think our own Social Style, whatever it may be, is the best. Our first tip: Remember, there is no evidence that any style is best or even better, even in a given situation. They're different. We are who we are, and we've all had our successes doing things the way we feel most comfortable doing them. The power of *Versatile Selling* is in accepting, understanding, valuing – and adapting – to those differences.

Identifying Social Styles will take practice. Five essential keys are:

1. *Don't jump to conclusions.* Don't make assumptions about the reasons for others' behavior. For example, if another person wants to get to know you before getting down to business, don't assume he or she is not interested in the task or is wasting time.
2. *Gather enough information to make accurate determinations of people's Social Styles.* A loud voice alone is not sufficient evidence you are dealing with a Driver or an Expressive.
3. *Accept people's behavior as a sign of their comfort zone and nothing else.* Thoughts and feelings are not part of Social Style analysis.
4. *Observe one dimension of behavior (assertiveness or responsiveness) at a time.* It's difficult to assess all behaviors and Social Style indicators at once. Break your observations into chunks. To evaluate on the assertiveness scale, ask, "Is this person more or less inclined to ask questions than I am when it comes to trying to influence people's thoughts and actions?" Your answer can locate someone to the left or right of the midpoint on the assertiveness scale, which narrows your decision to two choices. To the left, the person is either an Analytical or an Amiable. To the right, a Driver or an Expressive. To evaluate someone on the responsiveness scale, ask, "Is this person more or less inclined than I am to focus on the people on a team when it comes to expressing feelings about a project?" Your response will locate person above or below the midpoint on this scale. Again, this gives you two choices. Above the midpoint a person is more task-directed – an Analytical or a Driver. Below the midpoint,

the focus is more people-directed – an Amiable or an Expressive.

5. *Observe verbal and nonverbal behaviors – and be objective.* If you tend to smile when meeting someone new, don't immediately assume a serious-faced, stern-voiced sales prospect is unhappy, unapproachable, or dislikes you. Use Social Styles to understand that this person may be a Driver or an Analytical. Read the body language. Listen for word choice and voice inflection. Ask yourself, "What is this person telling me about the way he or she likes to do business?" This prospect may be looking for data or quick insights about the results your product or service has to offer. The smiles will come later as your relationship evolves.

6. *Ask targeted questions.* To identify Social Styles for yourself and others, ask questions about traits from the four matrix quadrants.

ASSESSING STYLES BEFORE YOUR FIRST MEETING

How can you prepare for a first contact with a customer when you don't yet know his or her style?

- Get as much information that is style-related as you can from the referral person or a mutual acquaintance.
- Ask your referral person about the customer's habits and characteristics (e.g., "Does she tend to speak fast or slowly?"). The referral person may not know about Social Styles.
- As you ask, keep in mind the style of the referral person. To an Expressive, another Expressive doesn't necessarily speak fast.
- If you don't get enough information to pin down a specific social style, try at least to determine one of the two dimensions.

At your first meeting, if you don't know your customer's style, use opening communications that address the needs of all four styles. For example, ask "How are you today?" and let the customer choose how far to carry that question (to see how people-oriented he or she is). Come with an agenda – but don't bring it out until you sense it will be welcomed by task-driven customers. Plan to finish on time or early, to satisfy task-driven customers. If you are making a presentation, include some "eye candy" for a potential Expressive.

You may not have the opportunity to conduct complete interviews with customers for the sole purpose of figuring out their Social Styles, but working these kinds of questions into your conversations helps:

- Will you be working with several other people on this project, or by yourself? (Listen for comfort or discomfort with this arrangement.)
- Will this decision be made by you, or will you get others involved in the process? (Listen for comfort or discomfort with this choice.)
- How will you create the project team? How will they make decisions?
- What do you like best and least about your job? Why?

All of these Social Styles tips and tools are intended to help you communicate more effectively – and *appropriately* – with customers of all styles. As long as customers are doing the buying and we're doing the selling, you can be sure it will remain up to us to adapt to make sure communication in the selling process goes smoothly.

Have you figured out where you fit in the Social Style matrix? Check out your assumptions with people who know you. The Social Style Profiler on the next two pages will give you some practice.

Whatever your Social Style, learning to modify your behaviors will reduce relationship tension, help you gain commitment, and increase productivity in your sales relationships. Now you are ready to explore Versatility with Analyticals, Drivers, Amiables and Expressives.

SUMMARY
- The four Social Styles – Analytical, Driver, Expressive and Amiable – are based on two million profiles worldwide. They help us understand and appreciate differences, not make judgments about people.
- To avoid habitual responses to behavior we see, we need to focus

only on observable behavior, not the thoughts, feelings, character or personality of others.

- Gesture, body position, tone of voice, facial expression, focus on facts or feeling are what we must "read."
- People are inaccurate in identifying their own Social Style 70 percent of the time but that's less important than identifying the Social Style of your customers.
- You *cannot* and *should not* feel you must move outside your own Social Style and comfort zone. Rather, you should adapt your natural behavior to your customer's Social Style – which is Versatility.
- The world population divides equally into Analyticals, Drivers, Expressives and Amiables, so your behavior has a lot in common with 25 percent of all people.
- **Analyticals** are ask- and task-directed. They are reserved, want data, try to minimize risk, respect processes and plans, value being considered experts, and are misperceived as not having feelings or having fun.
- **Drivers** are tell- and task-directed. They are direct but restrained, results-oriented, decisive, take risks, like control and challenge, value power, and are misperceived as impersonal and pushy.
- **Amiables** are ask- and people-directed. They are warm, open, and like a slow, steady pace which allows relationships to develop. People, coaching, approval and shared responsibility are important. They are misperceived as not focusing on results.
- **Expressives** are tell- and people-directed. They are energetic, inspiring, emotional, intuitive, use gestures and their voices variably, like getting results through people, value recognition and uniqueness. They are misperceived as not being businesslike.
- To identify a person's Social Style, use a wide range of verbal and nonverbal information. Make no judgments.
- Observe one dimension (assertiveness, which is about the ask- or tell-orientation; or responsiveness, which is about the task- or people-orientation) at a time.

SOCIAL STYLE SELF-PROFILER

First practice profiling two or three people you know as examples for each of the four Social Styles. Then profile yourself and check your results with others.

People to whom this description applies:

_____

_____

_____

_____

ANALYTICAL

Reserved. Cool. Few gestures. Proper speech. Formal posture and appearance. Deliberate rate of speech. Detail-oriented. Deliberate. Well-organized. Listens to and studies information carefully before weighing all alternatives. Lets others take the social initiative. Prefers an efficient, businesslike approach. Prefers information presented in systematic manner. Conservative and practical in business decisions. Technically oriented. Relies on structural approach and factual evidence.

People to whom this description applies:

_____

_____

_____

_____

AMIABLE

Friendly and open. Relaxed posture. Slow speech. Pleasant and soft voice. Open and eager facial expressions. Warm. Cooperative. Attentive. Generally gathers information and processes it with others before making decisions. Wants to establish strong, trusting relationships. Wants decisions supported by others. Careful but cooperative. People-oriented. Relies on others. Prefers interactive problem-solving.

DRIVER

Serious. Formal posture. Restrained gestures. Rapid speech. Direct. Voice inflection varies little, usually only to emphasize important points. Seeks influence over tangible resources and decision making. Desires control. Results-oriented. Clear objectives. Responds to those who demonstrate results. High sense of urgency. Little need for establishing relationships. Knowledgeable and demonstrates leadership in business decisions. Goal-oriented. Relies on information that supports results. Acts quickly and confronts issues directly. Expects people to listen carefully and respond in a timely manner.

People to whom this
description applies:

_____

_____

_____

_____

_____

EXPRESSIVE

Direct and open. Energetic. Gestures that are open and wide. Voice that is loud and varied. Lively. Fast-paced. Outgoing. Enthusiastic. Has a vision of the future and is responsive to those who can help achieve it. Establishes open, trusting relationships. Collaborates in finding and implementing quality solutions. Sees the big picture before probing for details. Futuristic. Holistic thinker. Inspiring.

People to whom this
description applies:

_____

_____

_____

_____

_____

4 | Versatility with Analyticals

"In God we trust.
All others bring facts."

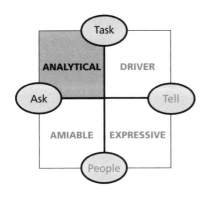

After his first exposure to Social Styles many years ago, Bob Davis couldn't wait to talk with his wife about what he had learned. He was excited and convinced that these new insights into how to communicate more effectively were going to profoundly influence his life and his work. Bob is a senior associate with McCourt Associates, a Wilson Learning business partner.

"I was determined as soon as I got home to demonstrate my new skills and knowledge. I told Madelyn everything I had learned about Social Styles. For my grand finale, I concluded my dissertation by *announcing,* 'Based on all this new wisdom *I* have, *you* are an Analytical.'

"She wasn't impressed.

"She asked, 'Do you have information to support that conclusion?'

"So I proceeded to *tell* her more of my reasons for my evaluation of her style of behavior. But I did not convince Madelyn of anything in that first conversation. What I wanted was an immediate conclusion. What she needed was time to process the information."

The Analytical Social Style

Detail-oriented. Deliberate. Well-organized. Listens to and studies information carefully before weighing all alternatives. Lets others take the social initiative. Prefers an efficient, businesslike approach. Prefers information presented in systematic manner. Conservative and practical in business decisions. Technically oriented. Relies on structural approach and factual evidence.

Verbal and Nonverbal Cues	Reserved. Few gestures. Proper speech. Formal posture and appearance. Listens well. Deliberate rate of speech.
Work Style	Fairly independent. Follows structured approaches.
Attitude about Time	"Take time to deal with matters objectively and logically. Move with deliberation."
Attitude about Accomplishment	"The process used for getting results is almost as important as the results themselves."
Attitude about Others	"Relationships take time to develop, and someone else will probably make the initial effort to make a new contact."
Natural Work Activity Strengths	Planning and organizing.
Personal Motivator	Respect: Seeks to enhance reputation as a technical expert by making the right decision in the right way. Values being recognized for accomplishments and respected for expertise.
Common Misperceptions about Analyticals	No feelings and no ability to have fun.

The irony of this situation eventually hit Bob full force. "In that stage of my career I tended to perceive Analytical buyers to be resistant or difficult people. From my perspective, they asked endless questions and seemed as if they would never make decisions about anything. So I pushed harder. In hindsight, I realized it was often my relentlessness in trying to get commitment that pushed Analytical customers to be indecisive." And so it was with his wife.

"I was really enthusiastic about what I had learned. Despite my new Social Styles insights, though, I slipped into my old comfortable way of doing things. I wanted to simply dump the data on Madelyn and get the reaction I was after."

An important lesson in the Bob and Madelyn story: Using Social Styles as a foundation for Versatility in sales takes practice and patience. *Understanding* and *implementing* are not the same thing.

There are many other lessons to explore specifically related to Analytical customers, and that is what's coming up in this chapter. Take a moment to review the Analytical Social Style chart on page 67, and then we'll move on with the business of adapting your style so Analyticals say "Yes!"

ANALYTICAL EXPECTATIONS

Just about anybody will tell you that being passionate about what you sell is critical to success in sales. As is the case with all behaviors when using Social Styles tools, however, you must be selective in how you express your passion. If you act too tell-assertive or even too personal with Analyticals, you run the risk of coming across as unprofessional. That, of course, is one of the quickest ways to make an Analytical uncomfortable. Enthusiasm doesn't sell well with them. You'll be more likely to ease relationship tension with an Analytical by initially being moderately cordial (but not chummy), and being diligently prepared to deliver a businesslike presentation based on well-organized, well-researched, expert-driven data.

Save the conversation about holiday travels or children's teams or hobbies. Your relationship with an Analytical might evolve to the point where such conversations eventually may be well received or even desired. In most instances, however, it pays to get to the point with people whose behaviors fall into this ask-directed, task-directed quadrant of the Social Style matrix.

Analyticals expect you to:

- *Adopt a predictable, task-oriented approach with them.* They are naturally most comfortable when they can operate with a high degree of objectivity.
- *Be well prepared.* Double-check every fact, every number, every person's name and title. You would do this anyway, but with an Analytical such errors can damage your credibility on a much higher level.
- *Be focused.* Carefully organize your presentation to make sure it is entirely pertinent to the task or problem you are discussing. Analyticals don't want all the data, they just want all the relevant data.
- *Be deliberate but flexible.* Analyticals like to see the process move along at a deliberate pace, but they also want sufficient time for thoughtful consideration of the key points being explored.
- *Offer quick confirmation of the expertise you and your company bring to the situation.* Analyticals want to feel confident you can provide factual information worth weighing.
- *Submit well documented, detailed information.* When you think you have provided all the information there is, some Analyticals will be just warming up to ask for more. Usually, delivering data effectively is the only kind of interpersonal assurance Analyticals require. Respect is their measure of personal value – respect for authentic data and for expertise, logically presented.
- *Support their principles and reasoning.* By the time you meet with Analyticals, they will have done much work and preparation related to the challenge you hope to address with your product or service. Your presentations to Analyticals should be consistent with how

they view their problems. Assure them you will follow a step-by-step process that will guarantee the strongest possible solutions.

- *Furnish solid evidence to help them make up their minds.* Analyticals want you to provide as much relevant, accurate data as they need to feel they are making completely informed decisions. If you can provide follow-up service, put it in writing.

RELATING WITH ANALYTICALS

One of the four main obstacles to buying – and selling – is lack of trust, comfort and confidence. In Wilson Learning's Counselor selling process, we recommend dealing with this issue in the first stage of the sales process. We call this stage Relating. If you use a different process, just substitute your terminology for this critical step.

As we discussed in Chapter 2, Relating is focused on building credibility with customers. Your ability to create credibility is influenced by *Propriety* (your dress to your language), *Competence* (your ability and background), *Commonality* (your shared values and experiences), and *Intent* (your dedication to serving the interest of the customer). The main challenge many salespeople face in building trust with new customers is to not rush through this stage with the idea of closing out a transaction as fast as possible. Versatility requires us to slow down, understand the Social Style of the customers, and make a deliberate effort to relate to them in the ways in which they feel most comfortable getting to know a new business partner.

In the Relating stage with Analyticals:

- Research their situation and needs as thoroughly as possible before you meet, and be prepared to demonstrate the knowledge you and your company offer. Search for articles on the Internet. Visit the company's website. Look for items in the local newspaper or its website. Talk to colleagues, friends, associates in professional organizations who might know anything about the industry sector, company or the individual customer. Then get ready to show how your product or service will address your customer's needs.

- Ask and confirm the time and location available for your meeting.
- Provide background information about yourself, your company, and your expertise.
- Don't open your meetings with small talk and self-disclosure.
- Slow down. You're providing a lot of information. Make certain you allow time for pauses, reflection and questions. When you ask a question, if your customer doesn't answer right away, try not to speak just because the silence may feel uncomfortable. Wait for the carefully considered reply or a clarifying question, in the thoughtful pace and rhythm with which Analytical customers often feel most comfortable.
- Ask about the customer's business concerns, and listen (as difficult as it may be), without interrupting.
- Structure your Purpose, Process and Payoff statements (also described in Chapter 2) about your meeting to suit ask-directed, task-directed behavior preferences.

Your first challenge in Relating with an Analytical might be getting an appointment. Consider sending a businesslike letter that provides some of the details recommended above. Once you are in the door, approach an Analytical customer from an advisory role, but also make a point of recognizing the customer's "expert" status.

Prove you have done your homework about the customer and the company. Offer specific evidence of where you have provided help in similar situations. But be very conscious of time.

DISCOVERING WITH ANALYTICALS

Discovering is perhaps the most critical step in the sales process. It is in this stage that you learn about the customers' needs, uncover the root causes of their problems, and determine if your products or services provide a viable solution. This is when you establish the need for what you have to offer.

In the Discovering stage with Analyticals:

- Ask specific fact-finding questions.
- Proceed in an organized and systematic manner.
- Listen to and note the details, even if you're hearing more than you want to know.
- Set a slow, thoughtful, unhurried pace.
- Be thorough, but not redundant. The last thing you want an Analytical to think is that he or she has answered the same question twice.
- Let your customers know you are aligned with their thinking and can support their business objectives.
- Encourage some discussion of ideas and feelings to provide balance to the factual information, but orient that discussion to the tasks or business problems with which your customer is concerned.

Keep in mind that you are striving for a comprehensive exchange of information in this stage. The payoff for your diligence in Discovering will come when you must justify your recommendations about your products or services, and when you have to handle objections.

Also, remember to refer back to Chapter 2 for specific recommendations on questioning and listening skills that will help in Discovering – permission questions, fact-finding questions, feeling-finding questions, best-least questions, magic-wand questions, tell-me-more questions, and catch-all questions, as well as responsive listening and restatement and checking techniques.

ADVOCATING WITH ANALYTICALS

In the competitive marketplace in which we now all operate, customers know they have many options for products and services similar to yours. This may be especially true of Analyticals because of their attention to data and details and their desire to do thorough research on every project. That is why it is so critical during the Advocating stage to develop your customer into as strong a believer in what you sell as you are yourself.

This is the stage in which you present your solutions, based on what you learned during the Discovering stage, and ask to close the deal. Your job now is to describe what you have to offer, clarify how it resolves the customer's problem, and spell out the benefits.

In the Advocating stage with Analyticals:

- Provide a detailed written proposal for your recommendation, but make sure you present it in person, if at all possible. If you can't do so, consider a teleconference or webcast.
- Recommend a specific course of action.
- Make sure your proposal includes the strongest possible cost justification or risk reduction.
- Clearly present all your assumptions, numbers and how you arrived at them.
- Make your presentation organized, systematic and precise.
- If you are unable to answer a specific question, offer to find the answer and come back with the information.
- Be reserved but not cold, decisive but not aggressive.
- Limit your use of emotional appeals.
- Limit your use of references to "others who are doing it" as evidence of the viability of your solution.
- Provide an opportunity for a thorough review of all documents related to the purchase and delivery.
- Ask for the order directly, but be low-key.
- Expect to negotiate changes in details in your standard contracts and other paperwork. Analyticals will need you to think quickly through how you can modify elements of your agreements to meet their specific requirements.
- Pay special attention to pricing issues.
- Cite supporting data that stresses your company's record and service capabilities.

It is extremely helpful when Advocating with Analyticals to work toward coming to complete commitment at the time you are asking for the sale. Make sure you have provided enough accurate information that there will be no need for delay or additional data gathering. Be careful, however, not to rush the decision-making process or to set unrealistic deadlines. Don't build in any tricky-sounding incentives for Analyticals (like "sign here, today, and get an extra discount"), and stay away from using gimmicks or clever, quick manipulative closing techniques.

SUPPORTING WITH ANALYTICALS

Yogi Berra, the famous catcher for the New York Yankees baseball team, renowned for his malapropisms and folksy intelligence, once said, "It ain't over 'til it's over." In customer interactions, it's never over. And you don't want it to be. Research shows that profitability from satisfied, loyal customers can be doubled by post-sale activities. They are a valuable resourse.

As described in Chapter 2, there are four pillars of the Supporting stage of the sales process, all of which are targeted at assuring customer satisfaction with the purchase.

Although Supporting is technically the final follow-up stage in Wilson Learning's four-step Counselor sales process, the work of guaranteeing satisfaction actually begins before a contract is signed or a check is mailed.

In the Supporting stage with Analyticals – *before* delivery and implementation:

- Provide a detailed plan for the delivery and implementation process in writing.
- Clarify the roles and responsibilities of everyone involved, including your own people.
- Coordinate the resources that will be applied during the implementation of the solution.

The Four Pillars of the Supporting Stage of the Sales Process

Supporting the Buying Decision	This can begin before the contract is signed. Look for signs of "buyer's remorse" or last-minute uncertainty. Support is also important after the sale.
Managing the Implementation	Customers can get nervous if you hand them off to someone else for implementation after the sale. Make the transition seamless.
Dealing with Dissatisfaction	Don't look for blame if things go wrong, just make things right. Recovering quickly from post-sales problems can actually increase overall customer satisfaction and strengthen your relationships with buyers.
Enhancing the Relationship	When things go well with sales, look for other ways to serve those same customers. It's easier than finding new ones.

In the Supporting stage with Analyticals – *after* the purchase and delivery of your product or service:

- Put the customer in direct contact with any technical experts involved in the implementation or support process.
- Provide accurate, periodic reviews. Putting them in writing may be most effective.
- Limit the frequency of your follow-up calls. There is a fine line between being thoroughly supportive and bothersome.
- Provide data on product or service updates, including any news about industry trends and research.
- Provide a summary of costs and benefits over the life of the product or service.

- Provide detailed replacement or de-implementation plans and schedules.

Remember that just before and just after a purchase, anxiety levels are likely to peak for your customers. Their concerns about profits, costs and performance will be at their highest point. Your job is to help ease those concerns. With Analyticals, the numbers and the details are a soothing tonic.

ADAPTING YOUR STYLE FOR ANALYTICALS

One of the most important things to remember about adapting your Social Style is that at times the effort might make you a bit uncomfortable. After all, three out of four of your customers probably fit best in a Social Style different than yours.

Whatever your style, when dealing with Analyticals, you need to be thinking about how to use more ask-directed and task-directed behavior. Your goal is not to "become" an Analytical, if you are not one, but to adjust your style to theirs.

The central theme in increasing ask-directedness is quite logical: Ask more, tell less. No one enjoys being pushed into decisions, especially Analyticals.

Naturally, you will have to do some telling to get your business done, but if you push too hard with Analyticals, resistance and relationship tension are likely to increase and productivity will drop. Therefore, with Analyticals:

- *Ask for the opinions of others.* Make a point of asking plenty of questions. Let the customer and other stakeholders in the process express their ideas. The most productive thing you can do with Analytical customers is to ask questions aimed at understanding their needs and helping them get a clear picture of possible solutions.
- *Negotiate decision-making.* It's not enough to just let customers have their say. Analyticals will tend to express their personal perspective

Checklist for Adapting Behaviors toward Analyticals

Try . . .	Avoid . . .
Preparing your case in advance.	Being disorganized or messy.
Sticking to business.	Spending much time on personal issues.
Supporting their principles. Use a thoughtful approach. Build your own credibility by listing the pros and cons for any suggestion you make.	Rushing the decision-making process.
Making an organized contribution to their efforts. Present specifics and do what you say you can do.	Being vague about what's expected of you or the customer, and not following through on what's expected of you.
Drawing up a scheduled approach to implementing a step-by-step action plan. Assure there will be no surprises.	Leaving things to chance or luck. Don't surprise customers with new approaches to which they have not previously agreed.
Following through, if you agree.	Providing personal incentives.
Making an organized presentation of your position if you disagree about what will best serve the customer.	Using gimmicks or clever, quick manipulations.
Giving them time to verify the reliability of your actions. Be accurate and realistic.	Using unreliable sources. Being haphazard.
Providing solid, tangible, practical evidence.	Using someone else's opinion as testimony or evidence.
Providing time for thoroughness, when appropriate.	Pushing too hard or being unrealistic with deadlines.

couched in terms of objective data or technical issues. You need to listen for the feelings under the facts. It's vital to good communication with Analyticals that you acknowledge and value their unique point of view and expertise.

- *Listen without interrupting.* Patience is important, especially when dealing with people who are slow or reluctant to express their ideas, as Analyticals tend to be. Analyticals can also be very occupied by minute details. Don't interrupt or dismiss these fine points, even if they seem irrelevant to the sale at the time. Analyticals need to be heard.

- *Adjust to the time needs of others.* A good sense of timing is as important as a sense of urgency. Be sensitive to the fact that some Analyticals may want a fair amount of time to evaluate an idea and think it through completely. Provide that opportunity.

- *Allow others to assume leadership roles.* You have to take charge in a sales situation, but you must be careful with Analytical customers not to infringe on their leadership roles or to question their knowledge and capabilities. Let your Analytical customers help create the agendas for your discussions, and provide sufficient opportunities for them to guide your conversations with their questions.

The main objective in adapting your behavior to accommodate the task-directedness of Analyticals is also quite logical: Focus first and foremost on what has to get done. Be careful about how much emotion you display and how much attention you pay to the people side of the responsiveness scale. Take a serious, businesslike approach, without appearing cold or indifferent, using ideas, techniques, and approaches like these:

- *Talk less.* Fight any tendency you might have to monopolize conversation.

- *Restrain your enthusiasm.* If you show too much feeling you might come across as immature. Strive to display balance and self-control.

- *Make decisions based on fact.* It is important to operate based on what's going on in your head, not your "gut" when working with Analyticals – they prefer data to intuition. Learn to explain your recommendations by emphasizing facts and details.

- *Stop and think.* Don't be impulsive or hasty. Pause and reflect about important issues before speaking or acting. Make sure you're thinking logically.
- *Acknowledge the thoughts of others.* Focus your attention on the needs and expectations of Analyticals. If you are overly enthusiastic or expressive it can draw attention to you – the wrong place.

UNDERSTANDING AND HANDLING BACK-UP BEHAVIOR WITH ANALYTICALS

As described in Chapter 2, when tension in sales relationships reaches the point where customers are saying, "I can't take it anymore," they begin exhibiting Back-Up Behavior. You are now at the moment when Versatility is needed most urgently. Your customer has reached that point of "fight or flight."

Analyticals in Back-Up focus first on Avoiding Behaviors – flight. They manage excess tension by limiting their exposure to the stressful situation. The message you will get loud and clear is, "I don't want to talk about it now." It will be extremely difficult, if not impossible, to set up a meeting or to get a return phone call from an Analytical in Back-Up mode. If you do get a chance to meet or speak, this unhappy customer will cut the session short, be reluctant to answer questions, and refuse to make a decision about – or even agree to study – the solution you are recommending. You will find it helpful to return to Chapter 2 now and review the LSCPA section on pages 41 through 44.

The goal in adapting LSCPA for Avoiding behaviors is to *intervene*. Draw out your customers' feelings so that you can address issues in ways that will help release whatever tension has developed in your relationships. Once you have used this process to head off a Back-Up situation, you can again begin to focus on the business problem you are both trying to solve.

You will know you have helped restore comfort for Analytical customers when they return to their characteristic behaviors. It may take some time and patience, but it's worth the investment.

SUMMARY

- Analyticals are ask- and task-directed. They are reserved, want data, try to minimize risk, respect processes and plans, value being considered experts, and are misperceived as not having feelings or having fun.

- They expect you to be prepared, objective, focused, and have solid data which shows how your solution supports their principles.

- In Relating, the trust-building stage, give Analyticals time to absorb your data. Be businesslike, accurate, realistic.

- In Discovering, the problem-defining stage, be sure to be organized and listen carefully, understanding that risk is not comfortable for Analyticals.

- In Advocating, when you are aligning your customer toward the solution, make your proposal detailed, address risk and cost, show your assumptions, limit emotional appeals and use supporting data, not references. Don't rush.

- In Supporting the process, document your implementation plan in detail; bring in technical experts or updates as needed.

- Analyticals in Back-Up adopt Avoiding behavior, the flight response. You must intervene to draw out facts and feelings, acknowledge them, and allow time for open disclosure.

5 | Versatility with Drivers

Pessimism leads to weakness, optimism to power.

WILLIAM JAMES

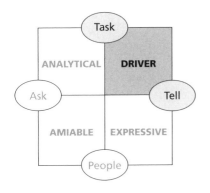

If you want to watch the classic Driver in action, get yourself a DVD or video-tape of the original version of the American television series *Dragnet*. In the series, Sergeant Joe Friday is a no-nonsense, staccato-speaking, earnest, hardworking police detective. In terms of his observable behavior, Friday is an extension of his creator, Jack Webb, who plays Friday in what's become a classic of American television drama.

More than 20 years after Webb's death, Joe Friday is still one of the most famous and successful television police characters ever developed. There are books and dozens of websites dedicated to the program, the man, and even *Dragnet* memorabilia. In 1987, Universal Studios released a movie of the same title. And one of the major television networks introduced a new version of the *Dragnet* series in 2003, with the new Joe Friday modeled after the original.

Perhaps the most instructive aspect of watching Joe Friday to learn about Drivers is in reflecting on how this persona carried over to the perception of Jack Webb in real life.

Although Jack Webb was never profiled by Wilson Learning and thus we don't have objective confirmation of his Social Style, descriptions of his behavior by others point to the Driver quadrant. The press judged him quite harshly at times for his Driverish behavior, on and off-screen. As we have emphasized previously, however, it's most productive to think about Social Styles without attaching judgment. There is no good or bad style, just different. And there's no gain in making suppositions about the behavior you can observe.

Ben Alexander, a close friend and member of the Dragnet cast, once commented on Webb in an interview with *TV People* magazine (October, 1957).

"The truth is that Jack works hard. Very hard. But he does not work so hard to escape from unhappiness, as some writers hint. He works hard just because he likes to work. . . . Jack loves to work on TV and movies. That's all. It's an all-absorbing passion with him."

"He is a man of great interest and intense sensitivity to the world around him . . . and he always keeps busy. He just couldn't stand still, ever. He's too dynamic."

As for the press's observation that Webb the Driver was irritable, Alexander said, "It's not that he's moody. It's just that he is strictly business, and concentrates fiercely on the job at hand. He's not aloof; he's only preoccupied. He has a big job to do and wants to do it efficiently, quickly. . . . Around the set, Jack is quiet. He's not the practical-joker kind, although he enjoys a good story and can tell one, too. But he has no time for time-wasting horsing around. We know we're there for business, and we have a film to make, so we concentrate. There are no long delays, for the simple reason that Jack is the boss and everything is laid out efficiently for us. He's patient, when need be, but he makes quick decisions."

With Jack Webb and Joe Friday in mind, use the table on the next page to review the characteristics and behaviors of Drivers, then we'll move on with the business of adapting your style so you won't miss the opportunity to get more Drivers to say "Yes!" to your sales efforts.

The Driver Social Style

Businesslike. Results-oriented. Likely to take charge and take initiative. Likes challenges. Makes quick decisions. Direct and to the point. Strong opinions and convictions. Hard-working. Efficient. Confident and competent. Productively co-ordinates the work of others. Likely to challenge new ideas. Quick to respond. Inclined to correct, modify or add to others' ideas. Straightforward. Responsible. Makes things happen.

Verbal and Nonverbal Cues	Serious. Formal posture. Restrained gestures. Rapid speech. Direct. Voice inflection varies little, usually only to emphasize important points.
Work Style	Independent.
Attitude about Time	"Use it efficiently to get desired results."
Attitude about Accomplishment	"Achieve strong results in the shortest time possible."
Attitude about Others	"Relationships are important but secondary until a task is defined and competency to deal with it is established."
Natural Work Activity Strengths	Initiating and monitoring.
Personal Motivator	Power: Seeks to control the tangible resources of a project such as time, budget, people. Prefers to be given options and probabilities and allowed to make own decisions. Values receiving more authority, control or power over the situation or environment.
Common Misperceptions about Drivers	Impersonal and pushy because they focus on tasks and control their emotions.

DRIVER EXPECTATIONS

"Don't take it personally. It's only business."

If you are ever likely to hear those words from the lips of someone you know, they most likely will be spoken by a person whose behaviors are best captured in the Driver quadrant of the Social Styles matrix. Even the short, punchy sentences say "Driver."

If those two short sentences come to you as advice from a Driver friend recommending how you can sell successfully to another Driver, accept the recommendation. It is a sound suggestion.

The time you have to make a first impression with a Driver will be extremely brief, and your customer's reaction at the end of that time will be swift and decisive. Your prospects of doing business with Drivers are likely to fade quickly if you initially come across as making frivolous use of their time. Forget amiability. Stay away from any behaviors that might make you appear overly smooth, slick or glib. Don't rely on "relationship." No matter how careful you believe you are in nurturing personal connections, Drivers are perhaps the most difficult people to connect with on that level, at least in the initial stages of the sales relationship.

Get on quickly with the business of demonstrating that you understand and can address "the big picture," will act in ways that will have a positive influence on the customer's bottom line, and can get the job done on deadline. Stick to providing only the most relevant information. Drivers, like Analyticals, are task-directed, but unlike Analyticals, are not interested in understanding every nuance and every piece of data related to your product or service.

Don't misinterpret that characteristic of Drivers, however, to mean you don't have to worry about the details. In the end, you will have to be thorough, on target, and in control of every aspect of your project. If not, your Driver customers, who typically are not prone to reveal much about their thoughts or feelings through expressions or gestures, might become very demonstrative in showing you the way out of their offices.

Drivers can be charming, but most often people in this tell-directed, task-directed quadrant of the Social Styles matrix don't focus on presenting an air of friendliness, nor do they expect it from the salespeople with whom they deal.

So, be prepared, be well informed about the customer's company, and be ready to be challenged.

Drivers expect you to:

- *Be task-oriented.* With Drivers, business comes before relationships.
- *Make the most efficient use of their time.* Drivers tend to be busy people with tight agendas. Think of Jack Webb finishing an acting performance then quickly changing hats to become Jack the director, Jack the producer or Jack the film cutter.
- *Provide insightful information early in your sales process.* Drivers are very interested in facts and well-documented reasons why and how your product or service will solve their problems. These are people who are more rational than emotional. They want to learn about benefits, and they expect the information you provide will be germane and accurate.
- *Submit ideas or solutions that fit their problems.* Drivers have a strong grasp of what they need and want, and they expect your ideas to support their agendas. If your plan veers too far from what they have in mind, you must be prepared to show how your idea ultimately advances their purpose. They will want options to ensure that your solution performs to their specific requirements. It's not that they want to be unique. They want to enhance their need for power or control.
- *Offer options in a way that allows them to feel they are making the ultimate decision.* Drivers desire control and may balk if they feel you are questioning or threatening their power or authority in any way. You may typically come up with all the best ideas in the problem-solving process with Driver customers, but you are more likely to close sales with them if you can sacrifice a few strokes to your own

85

ego in order to make it clear they are in charge.

- *Provide them with the odds for success when you ask them to take risks.* Drivers thrive on control, so they don't want to be blindsided by something unexpected. They don't want to be overburdened with details about a project, but fair warning about how likely it is something could go wrong – and where that failure might lead – would fall under the heading of relevant information.

RELATING WITH DRIVERS

As we've said before, one of the four main obstacles to buying – and selling – is lack of trust, comfort and confidence. It is essential to deal with this issue very early – if not first thing – in your sales process. Wilson Learning's Counselor selling process labels this stage Relating.

However you refer to this step in your sales process, it is the time when you are focused on building credibility with customers, which, as we outlined in Chapter 2, is greatly influenced by *Propriety* (your dress to your language), *Competence* (your ability and background), *Commonality* (your shared values and experiences), and *Intent* (your dedication to serving the interest of the customer). Pace is important in this stage. Many salespeople are challenged in building trust with new customers because they want to rush through to the point of closing out a transaction as quickly as possible. The need for Versatility, however, requires us to make a deliberate effort to relate to them in the ways in which they feel most comfortable getting to know a new business partner.

In the Relating Stage with Drivers:

- Establish a quick pace from the moment you meet Driver customers. Don't, however, neglect to give sufficient time to build trust with them. This can be a challenging balancing act.
- Listen and focus your complete attention on the Driver's ideas and objectives.
- Present only factual evidence that relates to the Drivers' business

problem and the outcome you can promise. Focus on the benefits and outcomes, not the data.

- Punctuality will pay off for you with Drivers. Arrive on time. No, arrive a bit early. Begin on time. Stay on task. Finish on time. Better yet, end a bit early; it will earn you some extra points.

- Get down to business immediately. Avoid small talk.

- Be prepared to provide plenty of information, but give it out carefully. Present the most relevant material, then dole out additional ideas and data only at the request of the Driver customer. Drivers want to get to the bottom line quickly, but at times will want to know the factual basis for your plans and conclusions. Although early encounters with Drivers may focus on "the big picture," be ready to provide on demand the kind of detail you would normally have prepared for a meeting with an Analytical.

- Be personable, but keep your gestures and facial expressions to a minimum. Speak firmly, but strive for maintaining a level tone in your voice. Some Drivers appear almost deadpan and expressionless in a sales situation and they expect more or less the same thing from everyone else. Create an environment of reserve and relative formality.

In Chapter 4, Versatility with Analyticals, we suggested one of the best ways to get a first appointment to meet with those ask-directed, task-directed customers is to send a businesslike letter outlining some of the key facts and figures about your product or service. A Driver might not take the time to read an introductory letter. A better strategy is to make your first contact by phone, and then follow up with a letter.

Again, make this contact businesslike and to the point. Take only enough time to introduce yourself, explain the business problem you can help address, offer support materials you have, and ask for an appointment to talk further.

When you follow up with a letter, confirm the time, date and location of your meeting, and provide any of the materials the Driver would be interested in reviewing before you get together. Restate any results of your first call. If your Driver customer does not specifically request you send information before you meet, it can still be helpful to include the address for your website in your letter – if you have a site available that does justice to your product or service.

DISCOVERING WITH DRIVERS

Discovering is the second and perhaps most important step in Wilson Learning's Counselor selling process. However you label this stage, your job is to figure out your customer's needs, including the root causes of the problems that have caused them to want to meet with you. It's also the point when you determine whether you can truly offer a solid solution and, if you can, make your case for what you have to offer.

In the Discovering stage with Drivers:

- Ask questions that allow the Driver to direct the interaction. Questions such as "What aspects of the problem are most important to you?" or "What is your goal with this purchase?" will allow Drivers to get out important information quickly.
- Ask fact-finding questions that will help you understand what they value and reward.
- Clarify priorities.
- Make your line of questioning consistent with the objective of your sales call.
- Keep a fast pace and stay on time.
- Follow up immediately on any requests for additional information.
- Support their beliefs and decisions. Make it clear how you can have a positive influence on their goals.
- Clarify their expectations about next steps.

Remember to refer back to Chapter 2 for specific recommendations on questioning and listening skills for Drivers in the Discovering stage.

ADVOCATING WITH DRIVERS

Of all Social Styles types, Drivers are likely to be the fastest to seek a competitive alternative to what you offer – if the solutions you suggest in this stage don't make a quick, positive impression. They know there are many options in today's marketplace similar to what you sell, and they will make swift decisions about moving on if you don't prove you have done your homework well in the Discovering stage. A Driver tends to dislike reversing a decision, so do your best to keep in the running.

Up until this point in your sales process you have been working to uncover your Driver customers' needs. Now is the point when you present your product or service as the right choice and ask for the sale.

Your challenge is to move your customers to the point of believing in what you sell as much as you do.

In the Advocating stage with Drivers:

- Provide documented options that allow for comparison between the alternative solutions you offer and their probable outcomes.
- Offer the best quality, given the cost limitations.
- Be specific and factual, but don't overwhelm with details.
- Appeal to their need to take independent action. Drivers prefer to be forthright in their decision-making, so reinforce their perceptions of their strengths and capabilities.
- Summarize quickly. Allow them to choose a course of action. Highlight the options, and leave the final decision up to them.
- Be direct when you ask for the sale. Ask for the order in clear, factual terms.
- Be prepared to negotiate changes and concessions. Drivers sometimes attach conditions to sales.
- Offer time to consider the options.
- Anticipate objections in advance; you're quite likely to hear some. Come prepared with facts, figures, examples, case histories and references that can help address any reservations.

It might seem as if coming in the door and providing a ready-made decision would meet a Driver's need for speed, but be careful not to take decision-making options and powers away from this type of customer. Close every loophole. Make sure there are no clouds hanging over the project or the data. Offer your options – without any wildly speculative guarantees or promises. Then, step back to provide the space and time Drivers need to take control and make their decisions.

If a Driver says "Yes," fight the urge to slip into small talk as you wrap up your discussions in this stage. No matter how good you are feeling about the sale, it really isn't time to relax and act as if you have reached some new level of personal connection in this relationship. Gather up your materials, pack your briefcase, shut down your computer and head off to take care of the next steps in this project or your next piece of business without slowing down to socialize. That's what Drivers would do.

SUPPORTING WITH DRIVERS

If you need an incentive for providing great support after a sale, remember that in terms of time, money and energy it is much more expensive to find a new customer than it is to do additional business with an existing client. Although we describe Wilson Learning's Counselor selling model in a four-step linear progression, you should be thinking about the Supporting stage throughout the entire sales process to guarantee satisfaction all along the way. There are four pillars in the model for Supporting customers, and you will need to use them all with Drivers – before, during and after the sale.

In the Supporting stage with Drivers – *before* delivery and implementation:

- Act immediately on any commitments you make.
- Keep to the schedule and agreed-upon costs – no surprises.
- Make all your communication quick and to the point.
- Set and communicate checkpoints and milestones.

In the Supporting stage with Drivers – *during* and *after* use of your product or service:

- Check to make sure Drivers believe they are getting their money's worth. Are they satisfied with the value of what you are providing?
- Ensure that your product or service is delivering the promised results.
- Don't call, write or drop in to check on Drivers unless there is a real need to do so.
- If your product or services gets "used up" after the sale, provide Drivers a quick and cost-effective way to transition to whatever must come next.

The Four Pillars of the Supporting Stage of the Sales Process

Supporting the Buying Decision	This can begin before the contract is signed. Look for signs of "buyer's remorse" or last-minute uncertainty. Support is also important after the sale.
Managing the Implementation	Customers can get nervous if you hand them off to someone else for implementation after the sale. Make the transition seamless.
Dealing with Dissatisfaction	Don't look for blame if things go wrong, just make things right. Recovering quickly from post-sales problems can actually increase overall customer satisfaction and strengthen your relationships with buyers.
Enhancing the Relationship	When things go well with sales, look for other ways to serve those same customers. It's easier than finding new ones.

- If disposal of your product is required after use, provide options and alternatives for how that can be accomplished most efficiently.
- Make things easy for Drivers and their staff members. Avoid getting them over-involved in whatever you must do to support the use of your product or service.

This four-step sales process – Relating, Discovering, Advocating, Supporting – is all about making your customer comfortable and confident with what you have to offer. Perhaps the most important things to remember in selling to Drivers are to be quick, clear, and on target.

ADAPTING YOUR STYLE FOR DRIVERS

At this point you should be feeling somewhat comfortable with your understanding of people who are Drivers. Don't forget, however, your Versatility challenge is to use that knowledge to make your customers comfortable. So, wherever your normal behaviors fit in the Social

Actions for Being More Tell-Directed on the Assertiveness Scale	
Get to the point	Simplify and clarify your opinions. Don't be vague or ambiguous in an effort to be tactful. Say what you mean. Be clear where you stand.
Volunteer information	Don't wait for others to take the lead. Express your opinions.
Be willing to disagree	Don't worry about conflicting with your customer's point of view. It's okay to disagree, as long as you do it without getting defensive or letting the challenge become personal.
Act on your convictions	Take a stand. Make decisions quickly.
Initiate conversation	Take the lead on introducing ideas and solutions.

Checklist for Adapting Behaviors toward Drivers

Try . . .	Avoid . . .
Being clear, specific, brief and to the point.	Rambling on or wasting time.
Approaching them in a straightforward, direct way – sticking to business in a pleasant but professional manner.	Being demonstrably excited, casual, informal or unprofessional.
Coming prepared with objectives and support materials in a well-organized package.	Forgetting or losing things, and doing things that confuse or distract.
Presenting the facts clearly and logically and planning your presentation for efficiency.	Leaving gaps or cloudy, uncertain issues.
Asking specific "what" questions.	Asking rhetorical or irrelevant questions or repeating them accidentally.
Providing alternatives that allow them to make their own final decisions.	Arriving with a ready-made decision that you've made.
Providing facts and figures related to the probability of success and the potential effectiveness of each of the options you propose.	Wildly speculating or offering guarantees and assurances that you risk not being able to fulfill.
Taking issues with the facts, not the person, if you disagree on something. Supporting the results, not the person, if you agree.	Letting a disagreement be reflected on a personal level.
Motivating and persuading by referring to objectives and results that your customer has identified previously.	Trying to convince by personal means or emotional appeals.
Departing graciously after finishing your business.	Telling stories and getting chummy after finishing business.

Styles matrix, you've got to be aiming for conduct that accommodates those who are tell-directed on the assertiveness scale and task-directed on the responsiveness scale.

What's the main strategy for moving your own behavior more to the tell-directed side of the assertiveness scale? Fewer questions, more answers. Tell more often. Ask less often.

The main strategy for being more task-directed on the responsiveness scale: Focus on what must get done, with as little emotion as possible. Allow your customer to take the lead on moving toward more personal topics. Task-directed people (the Drivers and Analyticals) do talk about personal things, but usually after they feel that the task has been dealt with. Let Drivers decide when the task issues have been completed.

Salespeople who are Amiable or Expressive try to influence with expression and feelings. Drivers often perceive this as the behavior of someone who is too emotionally involved in a situation. To influence Drivers, you must use a businesslike approach. You must be serious, but not appear cold or indifferent. To further increase the comfort of Drivers:

- *Talk less.* Don't monopolize the conversation. Learn to listen more.
- *Restrain your enthusiasm.* Drivers sometimes see excessive displays of emotion as a sign of immaturity. Strive for balance and control.
- *Make decisions based on facts.* It doesn't pay with Drivers – or Analyticals, as you learned earlier – to operate on "gut feeling" or instinct rather than logic. Use your head. Explain your recommendations using facts for emphasis.
- *Stop and think.* You need to be quick, but not impulsive or hasty. Pause and reflect on important issues before acting or speaking. That will help keep your emotions in check.
- *Acknowledge the thoughts of others.* Zero in on the needs and expectations of Drivers. Recognize their good ideas in ways that show the relationship is not all about you.

UNDERSTANDING AND HANDLING BACK-UP BEHAVIOR WITH DRIVERS

If you are off track with Drivers, it won't take very long for them to reach that dangerous, tense point in the sales relationship where they are saying, "I can't take it anymore."

When it comes to choosing fight or flight as an option for relieving their tension in sales situations, most Drivers first opt for *fight*. They become Autocratic, confronting, demanding, focusing even more intensely than normal on the issue, and looking harder than ever for a rational explanation for the situation.

Drivers manage extreme tension in a sales situation by asserting more control. Their basic message to you will be, "I am not going to do it this way. If you can't do it my way, we're finished doing business."

Their tone may be righteous, imposing, and cold, and they will use rank and intensified reason to make sure you get the message they have no interest in letting you move the relationship forward. Their unwillingness to cooperate further in the sales process will be displayed for you in a way that has a definite ring of finality.

You've got your work cut out for you. It's time to turn back to pages 41 through 44 to review ways to adapt the LSCPA model for *neutralizing* when customers are in Back-Up.

Neutralize Drivers' tensions by letting them vent. Usually this sounds like a lot of task-directed demands ("Here's what you'll do to fix it. Call your warehouse now and get them to ship our order tomorrow, without fail."). Let them express their needs and expectations, and then use LSCPA to focus on how to accomplish what they want. They'll tell you the *what* emphatically. You need to get to the *how*. But you can't get to the *how* until you've let them vent.

As you use these tools with Drivers, remember they are controlling, forceful and results-oriented people. Whatever you do to recover and try to restore comfort for a distressed Driver, efficiency and effectiveness will always be important, as will a sense of urgency and a willingness to deal unemotionally with even the toughest issues.

SUMMARY

- Drivers are tell and task directed. They are businesslike, results oriented, like to initiate things and control situations, appear confident but don't show a lot of emotion, like power and options, and are misperceived as impersonal and pushy.

- They expect you to be serious, well prepared, efficient, and form their first impressions quickly. They need "the big picture" and prize rational benefits. Offer them options so they can feel their decision-making will lead to success.

- In Relating, the trust-building stage, keep a quick pace and get to the point, focus on benefits and outcomes, remain formal. Know your facts but don't dwell on details.

- In Discovering, the problem-defining stage, let your questions give the Driver the lead, clarify and prioritize, and keep the pace brisk. Show how you can help the Driver reach his or her goals. Follow up impeccably.

- In Advocating, when you are aligning your customer toward the solution, present options, give room for independent action by the Driver, and document your solutions' benefits over the competition. Anticipate objections.

- In Supporting the process, follow up on all your commitments, keep the process on schedule and budget, work to ensure satisfaction and minimize your customer's need to get deep into the details of the solution.

- Drivers in Back-Up adopt Autocratic behavior, the fight response. Neutralize their tension by letting them vent, listening for how you can set things right.

6 | Versatility with Amiables

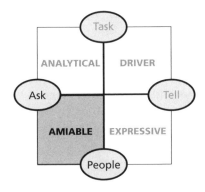

Selling to Amiables is an art unto itself. Their openness and interest in personal relationships makes them behave very collegially towards salespeople. Yet at times that sensitivity to others presents unique challenges as well. Thomas Koven is an instructional designer, facilitator and consultant who has worked with clients around the world as a member of Wilson Learning's extended enterprise. He has this tale to tell about selling to an Amiable customer.

"Our account manager and I had worked for close to three months trying to land a new piece of business with a major Canadian railroad. The customer had wanted a new approach to sales training that could be implemented system-wide. It represented a major change in their approach to their freight business. So we did everything we could to get it right for them. We spent extensive time interviewing different stakeholders to get a clear understanding of their business issues and requirements.

"Our customer contact, Eddie, was a very personable Amiable who was wonderful to work with. He was very open and cooperative with us and easily shared information or made necessary introductions within his company. We had put together a proposal that we thought exactly matched the customer's needs and fit within their budget parameters. And yet we couldn't seem to get the customer to commit. The buying decision was placed in a strange kind of limbo. 'We just haven't been able to make a decision, yet,' said Eddie. In spite of repeated inquiries we were unable to discover what was holding up the commitment.

"As I sat in the account manager's office, both of us staring up at the ceiling wondering what to do, I had an idea. Turning to my colleague, I said, 'What if we look at this from the perspective of Social Style?'

""What do you mean?' he asked.

"'Well, let's assume for the moment that there's nothing wrong with the proposal. In fact let's assume that we've got everything right.'

"'Okay,' said the account manager, 'so why don't we have the business?'

"'What do we know about our buyer?' I asked.

"'He's an Amiable.'

"'Right,' I said, 'and we know that Amiables value their relationships with their colleagues.'

"His eyes brightened. 'The buying committee!' he exclaimed. 'But we've interviewed them. We know what their interests are, and we've built them into the proposal.'

"'True,' I said. 'But now comes the moment of truth for Eddie. He's lying awake at night thinking, "If this doesn't work right, how will the others feel about me?" Amiables tend to be averse to risk, especially when the decision could jeopardize their relationships with others.'

"From this perspective my colleague and I brainstormed a number of approaches we could use to lower the risk of failure for our customer and protect his relationships.

The Amiable Style

Quiet. Unassuming. Supportive. Warm. Friendly listeners. Easy to get along with. Enjoys personal contact. Shares responsibility. Concerned about collaboration, providing support, and reaching agreement. Requires extensive data for decision-making. Prefers to have consensus before moving ahead. Often focuses on personal ties before goals.

Verbal and Nonverbal Cues	Warm, friendly and open. Relaxed posture. Slow speech. Pleasant and soft voice. Open and eager facial expressions.
Work Style	With others.
Attitude about Time	"Take time to establish relationships and to make steady progress through a slow, sure pace."
Attitude about Accomplishment	"Results come through people working together."
Attitude about Others	"People are the most important asset in any project and collaborating with others is the best way to get things done."
Natural Work Activity Strengths	Coaching and counseling.
Personal Motivator	Approval: Seeks to promote or gain agreement from others and to be included as part of the group or team. Values receiving others' approval and having a positive impact on others.
Common Misperceptions about Amiables	Places too much emphasis on relationships, move too slowly, and doesn't get results.

"The key to our strategy was to reduce risk and increase reassurance for Eddie. So we focused on the implementation plan. We recommended a phased rollout. It would begin with an initial pilot that would be followed by extensive evaluation and discussions with stakeholders, to ensure that everyone was comfortable with the final product. We asked for a commitment to the entire project, but promised continued consultation to guarantee that we were on the right track. We were confident that once implementation began, things would work out smoothly. The challenge was to help Eddie get past his initial Amiable concerns.

"Within a week we received a signed contract.

"Often in sales situations, we think we're covering all the bases, even the interpersonal dynamics between ourselves and our customers. Unfortunately, it is easy to forget the interpersonal dynamics within our customer organizations. Social Styles is a great tool for understanding this dimension of buyer behaviour and developing strategies for avoiding or overcoming these obstacles. With Eddie, we simply structured a Versatile response into our proposal – not to sell him, but to *help him buy*."

We all know Amiables, however, who are very successful and very effective at getting results in all facets of life, including in the business world. You learned the basics about this Social Style in Chapter 3. Take a moment now to review the chart on page 99. It provides a quick recap of how to recognize customers with this behavior style and will get you ready to learn more about adapting your style to get Amiables to say "Yes!"

AMIABLE EXPECTATIONS

You will probably never meet customers more willing to listen to you than Amiables, but you must take care with what you say, and how and when you say it. Amiables, even those with critical needs for your product or service, will want to get to know you personally before talking business. More than other styles, with Amiables, the need to know the people they do business with is as important as the product or service they are buying. You will need to sell yourself a bit before you can sell anything else.

Amiables will listen receptively, so plan to proceed slowly, and be certain to use some of that time to share information about you that goes beyond what would normally be considered "professional." Building relationships with Amiable customers is not about making friends, but it may feel that way at times if you follow their lead. Don't lose sight of your ultimate goal to solve problems and do business, but be prepared to open up and connect on a far more personal level than with customers of most other Social Styles.

This is the time, for example, to take note of the personal effects in a customer's office. If you see a photo of your client dressed in mountain-climbing gear standing atop a peak in the Alps or the Himalayas, and it has always been a dream of yours to climb Mt. Everest, mention that. Look for clues about your Amiable customers' personal lives. With a Driver you might just make a mental note about what those kinds of clues indicate about a person, but with Amiables bring them into the conversation. That will give your customers a chance to share more about themselves, but will also allow you to casually provide insights about yourself.

Amiables expect you to:

- *Be open and honest.* Amiables function well in situations where there are no hidden agendas, but they will be uncomfortable if you take a cold, get-right-down-to-business approach with them.
- *Spend time developing a relationship.* Amiables function best when there is little or no relationship tension by the time you begin to tackle the task at hand. They want to see progress toward goals, but are far more comfortable than Drivers and Expressives with moving ahead at a steady, deliberate pace.
- *Be congenial and prove you are trustworthy.* Establish your reputation with Amiables early in your relationship; it's something they value.

101

Don't rush your relationship or create too much pressure about the sale. That will cause Amiables to shy away from you.

- *Provide reassurance about who you are and what you believe.* Amiables are very interested in working with people who share their interests and challenges.
- *Give personal support.* Amiables look for signs of willingness to accept personal responsibility and provide personal support. They are not only buying a product, they are building a relationship. While written guarantees might be important to Analyticals, Amiables want the personal assurances from you as an individual. React and respond to their personal feelings and offer support and attention for the issues that matter to them most.
- *Provide guarantees and assurances.* Amiables are not risk-takers. They work deliberately and sometimes cautiously. Help them eliminate any worries they may have about the appropriateness of their decisions and the correctness of their actions.

RELATING WITH AMIABLES

Building trust with customers is always an important first step, but it is critical with Amiables, and it will take more than being able to establish the quality of your product or service. Relax. Be natural. Be patient. With Amiables it will seem like they are not very concerned about time and deadlines. But it is important to view time and deadlines from the Amiable's point of view. To an Amiable, you are saving time in the future by establishing trust early on. For Amiables, the pressure as deadlines approach is easier to deal with when they can trust, on a personal level, the people they work with, and with whom they have established a relationship that allows open discussion of issues. So, open up and use this warming-up period to let them know who you are – inside and outside of your role as a salesperson.

If you have any Driver tendencies, your greatest test with Amiables may be the need to hold back your desire for fast results.

In Relating with Amiables:

- Make "small talk." Engage in informal conversation before getting down to business.
- Ask questions about their work and personal goals. Listen actively to demonstrate a personal interest. Use plenty of facial expressions and body language that show your reactions to what you are hearing. Give verbal reactions. Ask clarifying questions that show you are paying close attention, and tie in some of your own experiences that relate to what you are hearing.
- If you have common acquaintances, mention them, especially if you have done business with those other people and can refer to them for testimonials about the quality of your products or services.
- Establish a slow, comfortable pace in your meetings. People come first with Amiables; tasks come next.
- Don't try to establish yourself or what you are selling as being revolutionary or cutting edge, or unlike anything anybody else offers. Amiables want to deal with products and services that are special, but even more important, they want to deal with people and products and services that have a solid reputation. They want to know you, and to be assured that what you offer as solutions has worked for others in the past. They want you to be there to support them if there are any problems. The message they like to hear is "others have tried this (or us) and are very happy with it."

A letter can be an effective tool for lining up a first meeting with an Amiable customer. As with everything else you do with Amiables, make sure this correspondence includes a personal touch. Mention those people you and the customer both know. Emphasize your personal reliability and your reputation for following through for your customers. Or find a way to draw a personal connection to the customers and their needs and the quality of your products or services.

Follow up with a phone call – a friendly call. Be open, honest and sincere. If there is no warmth in this contact, there's not much chance you'll get the chance to sit down to finally talk business.

DISCOVERING WITH AMIABLES

Amiable customers know that you need information from them in order to offer solutions for their problems. In fact, if you make the right initial impression, Amiables often will be very willing and intend to collaborate with you in completing this step in the sales process. But willingness and good intentions still don't mean the same thing as fast.

You may be eager to understand an Amiable's problems for all the right reasons – you want to help solve their problems, improve bottom-line results, or improve the quality of his or her life – but the relationship must still be attended to. Don't assume that you are not still Relating when you are doing Discovery.

Discovering, as you have learned earlier in *Versatile Selling*, and have no doubt experienced in your own sales career, is the most important stage of the sales process. You must have good information about customers' needs and circumstances in order to offer your best solutions. With Amiables, however, this exploration must include enough time for them to feel comfortable about the process of uncovering the personal factors that will influence the sales relationship.

Amiables are ask-directed, so you will have to dig for your information. First, though, you have to set the right personal tone.

In Discovering with Amiables:

- Use pacing, tone of voice, and body language to create a relaxed and cooperative atmosphere. Share information and feelings, and ask questions to get at the same for the customers. You want to create an open, warm exchange.
- Listen responsively. Give plenty of verbal and nonverbal feedback, especially when you hear information helpful in understanding the business challenges and issues you want to help resolve.
- Ask questions specifically related to achieving long-term goals. Amiables, who often are averse to risk and predominantly attuned to the present moment, tend to understate these kinds of far-reaching objectives.

- Verify if there are unresolved budget or cost-justification issues. Amiables are people-directed and ask-directed; financial issues sometimes don't automatically surface on their lists of concerns, so you must ask about any problems or limitations that might exist that would effect what you can offer.
- Find out who else will help make the buying decision. Amiables will frequently seek out quite a bit of support from within their organizations before making a decision or signing a check. If others will be involved in the final decision, you must also involve them in your process of Discovering the overall needs for your products or services.
- Summarize and feed back what you believe to be an Amiable's key ideas and feelings. Confirm you have understood and touched on the things most important to the client's situation.

Don't be surprised if an Amiable suggests you talk to others as well, and don't make the mistake of not following through. Amiables will want all opinions and ideas heard. Sometimes, when customers of other Styles suggest you do discovery with others, it can be an effort to "pass you off" to someone else. This is rarely true with Amiables. So if an Amiable suggests you meet with others or requests a group discussion, treat this as a positive opportunity to meet the Amiable's need for shared responsibility and collaboration.

ADVOCATING WITH AMIABLES

Amiables make specific decisions and close deals differently from the ways customers of other Social Styles do.

It's part of their strength that they are deliberate and effective at involving others in their projects. They coach. They counsel. They are supportive and helpful to others. They are loyal and dedicated to the people they work with, and are generous with doling out compliments and credit for the accomplishments and contributions of others. In turn, they look to colleagues to provide the same kind of help, support, and approval for their efforts.

For you, that means your selling process may be a bit more complicated. Don't oversimplify your reaction to what is happening. It's not that Amiables can't make decisions, or won't make decisions, it's that they make decisions only when they are confident of satisfying everybody who will be affected by them.

In Advocating with Amiables:

- Show how your recommended solutions will affect all the people involved with your project.
- Provide a clear rationale for why your solution to the problem is the best available now, and why it also will be the best in the future.
- Use references and examples of similar situations that turned out well in your presentation. Amiables take comfort in knowing you have dealt with their problems successfully before.
- Give guarantees. Provide contingency plans that will take into account as many likely scenarios as you can. Show Amiables how you can cover all the possible situations that might develop and what you can do to provide whatever protection could be needed.
- Ask for the order indirectly. Go easy.
- Support the Amiable's need to involve all those other people in the process of making a final decision. Allow yourself plenty of time for this phase of negotiations.
- Clearly define – in writing – who will do what and by when to move the process to a final decision and then to implementation. Spell out the details of your personal involvement in the overall project, the commitment of resources from your company and those required of the customer's organization, as well as the expectations for the Amiable's involvement in the completion of the process and project.
- Get a commitment, even if you have to get it based on a contingency. This will help keep Amiables from drifting away from making a final decision.

In Advocating with Amiables:

- Don't pressure them to make decisions.
- Don't corner them.
- Don't force them to respond too quickly. Avoid saying things such as, "Here's how I see it."
- Don't offer options and probabilities. They will foster indecisiveness.
- Don't position your product or service as something new or unique. Amiables typically don't want to be "the first" to try something. That indicates risk.

It's quite clear, especially if you are an Expressive or a Driver, that selling to Amiables requires a large dose of patience. It's equally important, however, to mix in a good-sized helping of persistence. If you truly have a product or service that will help Amiable customers be more successful, one of the most valuable things you can do for them is help keep the decision-making process moving. You won't be able to skip any steps or bypass any key people, but the faster you can provide the information and comfort Amiables require – for themselves and their fellow stakeholders – the faster you can help them close the deal in their own minds.

SUPPORTING WITH AMIABLES

Supporting is the final step in Wilson Learning's Counselor sales process, but everything you've learned so far about Amiables should be a good reminder this is not a linear model. We have presented the four steps throughout *Versatile Selling* in the most functional and most logical sequence, but Supporting can begin long before you ever close a deal. Indeed, with Amiables, it should.

The recap of the four pillars of the Supporting stage on page 108 provides a review that will be extremely useful as you prepare to support a project with Amiables.

The Four Pillars of the Supporting Stage of the Sales Process

Supporting the Buying Decision	This can begin before the contract is signed. Look for signs of "buyer's remorse" or last-minute uncertainty. Support is also important after the sale.
Managing the Implementation	Customers can get nervous if you hand them off to someone else for implementation after the sale. Make the transition seamless.
Dealing with Dissatisfaction	Don't look for blame if things go wrong, just make things right. Recovering quickly from post-sales problems can actually increase overall customer satisfaction and strengthen your relationships with buyers.
Enhancing the Relationship	When things go well with sales, look for other ways to serve those same customers. It's easier than finding new ones.

In the Supporting stage with Amiables – *before* delivery and implementation:

- Make them feel good about themselves for the decisions they have made. Congratulate them. Be aware that Amiables are quite susceptible to feeling "buyer's remorse," and it's part of your job to help get them through that phase.
- Help them sell their decisions internally. Amiables function best when they have support from key people in their organizations.
- Handle the details. Be mindful that Amiables are not big risk-takers and will want to be comfortable knowing every necessary step has been carefully considered, but taking care of those kinds of details themselves is not a strength or a preference.

In the Supporting stage with Amiables – *during* and *after* purchase and delivery:

- Assure that installation or implementation is correct and problem free. Provide periodic progress reports to show Amiables things are going well enough to keep everybody happy.
- Arrange for service contracts, training, or whatever else is needed to maintain their comfort, especially during the start-up phase.
- Work out any problems agreeably. Listen carefully to any concerns Amiables have, even if they seem trivial.

In the Supporting stage with Amiables – *after* completion or usage:

- If you are selling a product, make it easy to discard or upgrade after it is used up. Whether you are selling a product or a service, continue to provide information about new versions or modifications.
- Help them manage the change process that comes with using – or using up – your product or service.
- Continue to call or write messages that show your personal interest in their satisfaction and success. Some of these contacts could be tied to birthdays or as follow-ups to personal interests.

Every customer feels some anxiousness after making a buying decision, but Amiables are most likely to feel significant post-purchase fret. During the Supporting stage of your sales process, stick to what they value: Stay in contact, provide plenty of positive feedback, keep all the key players involved in the process. And make it feel personal.

ADAPTING YOUR STYLE FOR AMIABLES

Amiables are ask-directed on the assertiveness scale and people-directed on the responsiveness scale. As you strategize for adapting your behavior to make them comfortable in sales situations, think about the behaviors that demonstrate warmth, patience and persistence.

As you learned with Analyticals, the central theme in increasing ask-directedness is relatively simple in theory: Ask more, tell less. Amiables don't want to be rushed on their decision-making, and they don't want to feel as if you are pushing them into uncharted territory. As always, you have to get your business done, but proceed with patience and plenty of personal touches with Amiables or resistance and relationship tension are likely to increase. Therefore, with Amiables:

- *Ask for the opinions of others.* Make a point of asking plenty of questions. Let the customer and other stakeholders in the process express their ideas. The most productive thing you can do with Amiable customers is to ask questions aimed at understanding their needs and helping them get a clear picture of possible solutions.

- *Negotiate decision-making.* It's not enough to let customers have their say. When Amiables raise a point or offer a challenge, they're really looking for a chance to discuss their ideas and feelings from a personal perspective. Listen and respond to the feelings as well as the facts. It's vital to good communication with Amiables to acknowledge and value their views and expertise.

- *Listen without interrupting.* Patience is important. Like Analyticals, Amiables have a slower pace than Expressives or Drivers. In addition, Amiables value a supportive environment. If you interrupt, or in other ways make them feel rushed, they may very likely take it personally. Amiables will also be concerned with others' reactions, or with the effects of actions on others, and they will need to voice these concerns. Don't interrupt or dismiss these points, even if they seem irrelevant to the sale at the time. Amiables need to be heard.

- *Adjust to the time needs of others.* A good sense of timing is as important as a sense of urgency. Be sensitive to the fact that some Amiables may want a fair amount of time to evaluate an idea and think it through completely. Provide that opportunity.

- *Allow others to assume leadership roles.* You have to take charge in a sales situation, but you must be careful with Amiable customers not

Actions for Being More People-Directed
on the Responsiveness Scale

Verbalize your feelings	Talk openly about how you feel about the issues. You can establish better relationships by acknowledging your honest reactions.
Pay personal compliments	Sincere, legitimate compliments are always welcome by Amiables. Don't hesitate to state positive sentiments, or to find indirect ways to say good things about your customers.
Be willing to spend time on personal relationships	Pay attention to feelings. You may not see an immediate connection between personal involvement with Amiable customers and achieving sales goals, but friendship and sensitivity can build loyalty.
Make small talk; socialize	Amiables don't want communication with you to be "strictly business." Stay focused on your goals and objectives, but also talk about things that have nothing to do with business.

to infringe on their leadership roles or to call into question their knowledge and capabilities. Let your Amiable customers help create the agendas for your discussions, and provide sufficient opportunities for them to guide your conversations with their questions.

Comfort for Amiables also comes in working with salespeople who can adapt to their people-directed behavior tendencies. The main thing to remember with Amiables (as it is with Expressives, who are the other people-directed Social Styles group) is that they are looking for warmth, personal connections, and attention in their relationships.

It's hard to influence people-directed customers if you seem cold or impersonal, but it's also important not to overdo the personal connections. The chart below recaps key strategies and techniques for adapting behaviors for moving people-directed Amiables to "Yes!"

Checklist for Adapting Behaviors toward Amiables

Try . . .	Avoid . . .
Breaking the ice with at least a brief personal comment.	Rushing immediately to get into your business or address the agenda.
Finding areas of common interest as a way of showing sincere interest on a personal level.	Sticking coldly to business, but also avoid getting so personal that you lose sight of your business goals.
Being candid and open.	Having hidden agendas and appearing as if you are merely looking for an opportunity to move it to close the sale.
Talking about their personal goals – listening and responding with focused attention and energy.	Forcing the conversation toward quick decisions related to your objectives.
Presenting your case in a way that reflects your awareness and concern about related people issues.	Overusing facts and figures to support your case.
Asking "why" questions to draw out their opinions.	Being demanding or threatening with position power.
Watching for early signs of disagreement or dissatisfaction.	Manipulating them into agreements because you know they are not inclined to "fight back."
Acting casually and informally. Don't rush your movements.	Being abrupt and rapid.
Clearly defining – in writing – individual roles, responsibilities, and contributions.	Being vague or offering multiple options or probabilities.
Guaranteeing minimal risks, total satisfaction, and plenty of payoffs.	Making promises you can't keep; leaving them without ongoing support.

UNDERSTANDING AND HANDLING BACK-UP BEHAVIOR IN AMIABLES

The first Back-Up Behavior of Amiables is called Acquiescing. They manage stress and tension in their relationships by limiting their exposure to the cause of their woes. They opt to surrender or give up, which is their way of taking flight from the situation.

In a sales relationship, that means you may still get meetings with your unhappy customers, but you won't get the business. Amiables in the first stage of Back-Up may respond positively to you in these situations, even if they have made prior decisions not to accept your recommendations. They might even agree to a solution in a meeting to avoid creating new tension, only to retract the agreement later.

Their Ask-Assertive and People-Directed responsive nature creates two important points about Amiables in Back-Up. First, because of their Ask-Assertive tendencies, you might not notice they have entered Back-Up. All of a sudden they start agreeing with you, not showing tension in their actions or body language. But, because of their People-Directed responsiveness, they take conflict personally. If you keep Amiables in Back-Up too long (and when you don't sense they are in Back-Up, that is quite possible), you may never regain their trust.

Because Drivers and Expressives tend to fight in Back-up, you might feel that the worst you can do is get an Expressive or Driver in Back-Up. But the truth is, an Amiable in Back-Up can be more detrimental to your long-term prospects. An Expressive may explode in front of you, but will be more likely to forgive and forget. Amiables will tend not to forget, and if pushed far enough, will not forgive, ever!

The message you'll get from an Amiable who is Acquiescing is, "I give up. We will do it your way . . . until I get the chance to do it my way." That way begins the first moment you are out of sight.

You must decide then whether you will come back to try to salvage the relationship and potential sale. If you believe can make the save, step one is to refer back to the LSCPA tool described on pages 41 through 44 and work to *intervene* and reduce the customer's tension.

Determine what you need to do to begin your recovery. It's helpful to remember that, in most situations, Amiables are eager to develop solid, collaborative, personal relationships. Do whatever you can to reconnect to that core value and you will be on your way to resolving a tough situation. Getting through a crisis with an Amiable can actually enrich your long-term relationship.

SUMMARY

- Amiables are ask- and people-directed. They are quiet, warm, easygoing, open, like sharing responsibility and consensus, seek approval or agreement, and are misperceived as putting too much emphasis on relationships and moving too slowly toward results.
- They expect you to build a relationship before starting to do business, and appreciate warm, honest input. They want personal support, guarantees and assurances to limit risk.
- In Relating, the trust-building stage, they won't focus on deadlines and results immediately. Keep a relaxed pace, mention mutual acquaintances, and don't stress revolutionary attributes of what you sell, but rather reliability and proven success.
- In Discovering, the problem-defining stage, listen responsively and create a cooperative tone. Ask about long-term goals and budget issues and help make the buying decision a shared process.
- In Advocating, when you are aligning your customer toward the solution, expect Amiables to draw in others and seek their satisfaction. Use references, guarantees, assurances. Avoid pressing hard.
- In Supporting the process, help Amiables sell decisions internally, watch for buyer's remorse, handle details, provide progress reports. Work out problems pleasantly.
- Amiables in Back-Up adopt Acquiescing behavior, the flight response. You may not notice it because it's not openly tense, but it's dangerous because they take conflict personally. If trust is lost, it may not be recoverable. Try to reconnect to the core value of your relationship and intervene early.

7 | Versatility with Expressives

We are all worms. But I do believe that I am a glow worm.
WINSTON CHURCHILL

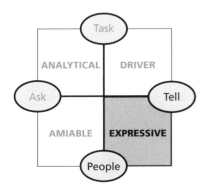

Expressive customers make for lively, challenging people to work with. Their quickness can make Analyticals and Amiables feel off-balance and decidedly plodding. Thomas Koven, a Canadian instructional designer, facilitator and consultant who works with Wilson Learning, had this experience with an Expressive client, Monique.

"Every consultant knows that we best serve our customers by making strong connections between our products and services to their business issues. We deliver value when our solutions solve problems.

"Imagine my surprise some years ago when I received a call from the new training manager of a long-standing client. Monique introduced herself briefly and confidently. Then she asked, 'So what do you have that's new?'

"'New?' I replied. 'What do you mean by *new*?'

"'You know what I mean,'" she exclaimed. "'New! Hot! What have you got that's leading edge?'"

"I floundered for a moment, wondering how I could answer this disconcerting request. And then I thought, 'Ask her some questions. Do some Discovering.'

"So I shifted into my best consultant mode and asked, 'Well, Monique, before I talk about what we have to offer, what business issues are you trying to resolve?'

"'Oh, never mind that!' she exclaimed, dismissing me. 'I just want to know what you have that's new. Don't tell me about what you've got now. Tell me what you've got in the pipeline that's exciting. That's what I'm after. Tell me that!'

"Have you ever noticed that however well we learn our lines, our clients never seem to learn theirs? Monique was an Expressive and I was trying to take a rational, deliberate approach with her. I wanted to talk about the present, but she wanted to talk about tomorrow.

"I gulped. I suddenly found myself pushed outside my comfort zone. Little voices inside my head began to chant, 'This isn't right! You can't conduct business this way!'

"But I could, and I did, because I suddenly recognized what my Expressive client was asking of me. Monique wanted me to take a little less plodding approach, with a broader scope and vision.

"The conversation that ensued was fast-paced, far-ranging, and even a little personal. We didn't discuss serious business issues then, but Monique was happy to talk about them in many subsequent ones. Reflecting on the exchange, I realized that I had successfully conducted a Relating call with Monique. Because she was new to her position and we had not worked together before, she just wanted to get to know me a little better. A reasonable request of course, but one made in her typical Expressive fashion."

Passion. Intuition. Creativity. Influence. When it comes to *Versatile Selling,* Expressives can be powerful allies if they believe in what you offer. Take a moment now to review the chart on page 117. It provides a quick recap of what you learned in Chapter 3 about customers with this behavior style and will get you ready to learn more about adapting your style to get Expressives to say "Yes!"

The Expressive Style

Energetic. Inspiring. Emotional. Fast paced. Comfortable taking social initiative. Engages freely in friendly conversation before tackling tasks. Futuristic. Talkative. Intuitive. Willingly shares ideas, insights, dreams and visions. Risk-taker. Competitive. Spirited. Creative. Enthusiastic. Likes an audience. Ambitious.

Verbal and Nonverbal Cues	Energetic and enthusiastic. Gestures that are open and wide. Voice that is loud and varied. Fast-paced and lively.
Work Style	With others.
Attitude about Time	"Move fast, but spend time energizing others, sharing visions, dreams and ideas."
Attitude about Accomplishment	"Get results through people."
Attitude about Others	"It is very important to work with people to help make their own dreams reality."
Natural Work Activity Strengths	Motivating and reinforcing.
Personal Motivator	Recognition: Seeks to be highly visible and to stand out from the crowd, to be seen as unique and showing leadership. Values recognition for accomplishment, publicity, symbols of accomplishment.
Common Misperceptions about Expressives	Flighty, more inclined to tell a joke than discuss a business issue. Not businesslike or task-oriented.

EXPRESSIVE EXPECTATIONS

Break out your best listening skills, and maybe even your most comfortable shoes, when it comes to doing business with Expressives. They are quick to speak, somewhat reluctant to give up the floor when they are engaged in conversation, and, when they are going full speed, not much inclined to listen – except perhaps to hear their own ideas confirmed.

You might also want to make sure you have an easy-to-read road map in mind for finding your way back from conversations that can take unexpected and off-the-business-path twists and turns. Every bend in your discussion with an Expressive matters, although at times it may seem as if they are expecting quite a bit of you to be able to keep up with their sweeping and far-reaching views of the world.

The comfortable shoes will come in handy if you happen to be standing, say, in the exhibition hall of a trade show, when your conversation begins. It could last a while.

Expressives expect you to:

- *Develop your relationship openly.* Expressives like to operate in a friendly, inclusive atmosphere.
- *Be tolerant of their casual use of time.* Expressives sometimes seem to deliberately cultivate a casual, relaxed approach without much regard for time. That often changes, however, when they are driving toward a goal. They don't worry much about the clock, until they have made a decision about what they want. At that point, they want rapid results.
- *Present "the big picture" first.* Expressives want to discuss and grasp the overall view of a situation before getting into the details.
- *Collaborate.* Expressives want you to work *with* them on proposing what will best serve their organizations.
- *Help them get a clear sense of who you are and how you do business.* Expressives appreciate dealing with people who are competent and confident. They will be impressed by solid references and will want to have contact information for others who have used and value your product or service.
- *Share sincere thoughts and feelings openly with them.* Expressives recognize others as being integral to reaching their goals, but they also

value people as individuals. They want to get to know you on a more personal level.

- *Provide them with recognition for their visions and actions.* Expressives want support for their ideas and decisions and will look to you for positive reinforcement. If you provide that support, it will add to an Expressive's perceived value of your relationship. Expressives want to like the people with whom they do business, and will be encouraged and pleased by your efforts to build a personal relationship.

- *Assure them you value and will implement their ideas.* Expressives want to be confident in the quality of work done and will be comforted when they see their passion and thinking translated into actions.

RELATING WITH EXPRESSIVES

Obstacle number one in sales: Lack of trust. Strategy number one to contend with lack of trust: Build credibility immediately in this stage in the sales process we call Relating.

Even though Expressives tend to ignore the passage of time when they are initiating relationships, it is important for you to be fast paced in establishing who you are, what you have to offer, and what the Expressives have to gain by inviting you into a relationship.

In Relating with Expressives:

- Quickly describe the purpose for your contact, whether it's a phone call, letter or face-to-face encounter. You are going to have to earn the right to develop a business relationship with Expressives.
- Share stories about people you both know.
- Share information that would be perceived as "exclusive."
- Share your feelings and enthusiasm for the goals and ideas of Expressive customers.
- Once you have established your competence and feel you have earned some initial confidence with Expressives, take some time to open up the relationship on a more personal level.
- Reinforce Expressives for their energy, vision and enthusiasm.

Generally, a phone call is the best way to make a first contact with Expressives. Be open, friendly, and stress the quick benefits, personal service, and experience you and your company can provide.

If you choose to use a letter or e-mail message to request your first meeting, make it short and personal. Explain who you are, what you know about the customer, and what you would like to talk about. Think "big picture" first, with details to come later.

DISCOVERING WITH EXPRESSIVES

Unlike when selling to Drivers, it won't take much effort to get Expressives talking about their needs and ideas. That's helpful because Discovering is the most critical work you must do in making a sale. Your goal is to get clear what the customer wants and needs. Uncover the problem. Establish where there is a need for an urgent solution. And begin to lay the groundwork for the solutions you can offer to deal with that problem.

Remember to turn back to the Discovering section of Chapter 2 to refresh yourself in the kinds of questions you can use in this stage of your sales process (permission questions, fact-finding questions, feeling-finding questions, best-least questions, magic-wand questions, tell-me-more questions, and catch-all questions). But, if you strike the right chord with Expressives in the Relating stage, you will have earned the right to hear what's on their minds, so it will be most important to be ready to listen and to use questions selectively to make sure you cover all the vital areas you need to understand.

In discovering with Expressives:

- Begin by asking about their vision of an ideal outcome.
- Identify other people who should contribute to the analysis of the problem and the planning of the solution.
- Listen, then respond with plenty of verbal and non-verbal feedback that supports their beliefs.
- Keep the discussion fast paced, focused, moving toward a result.

- Question carefully for the data you need. One challenge may be finding openings in an Expressive's side of the conversation where you can slip in inquiries. Be patient and alert.
- When the interest in the specifics of the situation wanes, summarize what has been discussed and begin to suggest ways to move the vision toward reality.

Expressives have a number of strengths that they are often willing to bring into play to help you in your sales process. They are typically open to sharing whatever information they believe you will need to meet the needs of their organizations. They will collaborate on creating the proposals you will likely need to prepare to make your sale; they see a value in helping make the proposal as effective as possible. Expressives will show their concerns about the quality of the solutions you jointly create, as well as for the implementation process, so there will be few mysteries about how they are feeling. When necessary, Expressives will also adapt to the needs of others, and they are willing to innovate and take risks.

All of these tendencies can be beneficial in your efforts to help Expressives get the internal support they need in order to move their relationships forward with you. Look for opportunities to engage those strengths as fully as possible.

ADVOCATING WITH EXPRESSIVES

If you are able to maintain Expressive customers' comfort through the Relating and Discovering stages, you are in good position to begin Advocating – to start moving them toward a commitment to a solution and the sale. You are ready to present the options you can offer, ask for a decision, and deal with any resistance that might exist.

In Advocating with Expressives:

- Provide specific solutions in writing. Take care to make sure your options reflect the ideas of Expressive customers, using their vocabulary, examples, etc. Build confidence that you understand their desires and have the necessary facts to offer a solution, but don't overwhelm them with details.

- Appeal to personal esteem needs. Help Expressives feel special in your dealings with them.
- Provide testimonials from people Expressives see as important or prominent.
- When you have enough information to have tested the appropriateness of your solution, assume the decision is made and ask for the order in a casual, informal way.
- Work to get final commitments to action in writing and make sure everybody is clear about the decision to buy.
- Save the details about the purchase until you have the firm commitment to buy. Expressives will be looking for you to handle this end of the deal.
- When the opportunity presents itself, offer something value-added or unique. Don't offer a price break unless you are sure it won't make your Expressive customer value your offering less. Rather, say, "Instead of red, with triangles, yours will be magenta, with circles and a bell." This can be part of making Expressives feel special.

A couple of behaviors to avoid when Advocating with Expressives:

- Don't confuse things by offering options.
- Don't rush the discussion. Spend time engaging your customer in developing ways to implement your plan.
- Don't leave buying decisions vague or unclear.
- Don't be curt or reserved.

As with Drivers, Expressives will ultimately hold you accountable for knowing all the details for whatever plans you agree to implement. It can be counterproductive, however, to spend time in the Advocating stage to present excessive facts, figures, alternatives and abstractions.

Your challenge with Expressives is to understand and agree upon "the big picture" to the point that you have earned enough trust and confidence to close a deal. As always, don't lose track of the details. Come back to them when you have locked in the commitment to complete the purchase.

SUPPORTING WITH EXPRESSIVES

Although we may be inclined to believe "support is support is support" when it comes to taking care of customers after a sale, Versatility is as much required in this stage as it is in Relating, Discovering and Advocating. The rules of Social Styles still apply, because people stay more or less consistent in Style, regardless of the circumstances.

We really are creatures of habit. This is born out by the fact that often when we profile people who have been profiled before, their Style remains the same or similar, even though years may have passed and they may have changed roles or even companies. You can count on people to behave in a consistent manner according to the dictates of their style. Thus when it comes to Supporting, knowing that you are working with an Expressive is very helpful because it allows you to predict or anticipate their style needs in this phase of the sale.

In addition to the prospects of doing more business with an existing satisfied customer, there is incentive for you to be especially attentive to Expressives in this stage of the sales process. They are perhaps most likely to voluntarily spread the good news about you, your company, and your products or services if they are satisfied with what you do for them. That can lead to sales inside and outside their organizations.

In the Supporting stage with Expressives – *before* delivery and implementation:

- Reconfirm the schedule.
- Find a way to highlight the personal aspects of the relationship you have developed.

The Four Pillars of the Supporting Stage of the Sales Process

Supporting the Buying Decision	This can begin before the contract is signed. Look for signs of "buyer's remorse" or last-minute uncertainty. Support is also important after the sale.
Managing the Implementation	Customers can get nervous if you hand them off to someone else for implementation after the sale. Make the transition seamless.
Dealing with Dissatisfaction	Don't look for blame if things go wrong, just make things right. Recovering quickly from post-sales problems can actually increase overall customer satisfaction and strengthen your relationships with buyers.
Enhancing the Relationship	When things go well with sales, look for other ways to serve those same customers. It's easier than finding new ones.

- Personally introduce the individuals or teams that will handle implementations and encourage them to establish productive working relationships. Use this period to further establish yourself and your implementation staff as part of the customer's team.
- But while introducing the implementation team, express your desire to stay close to the implementation and take personal responsibility for it.
- Help get the details sorted, organized and well in hand to serve whatever purpose will be required within your customers' organizations.

In the Supporting stage with Expressives – *during use* of your products or services:

- Be proactive in resolving any usage problems. Look for ways to make things easier for your customers.
- Handle any complaints personally, even if they relate to parts of the implementation for which you are not technically responsible. Don't delegate this problem solving unless you get your customer's permission to do so.
- Take your customer's lead in planning more social, informal contacts. If your customer suggests lunch or dinner meetings, use these as opportunities to develop the relationship and the business.

In the Supporting stage with Expressives – *after use* of your products or services:

- Inform Expressives of new, different, breakthrough products and/or services you may have to offer since the original sale.
- Celebrate. Take time to recognize completion and success with your Expressive customers. Expressives, more than other Styles, value the more tangible representations of a successfully completed project. Mementoes, personalized cards and small gifts to symbolize the success and the relationship can count for a lot.
- Align any potential follow-up business with changes that may have occurred in the original vision.

Expressives tend to be futuristic and holistic in their thinking. The Supporting stage is the time when you want to be asking and thinking about, "What's next?" If you meet or exceed expectations with Expressives, they are going to want to talk about that success and be in the frame of mind to expand their ideas about what else they can do to be successful.

ADAPTING YOUR STYLE FOR EXPRESSIVES

Comfort for Expressives comes from working with salespeople who can adapt to their tell-directed, people-directed behavior tendencies.

On the people-directed side of that equation, the main thing to remember with Expressives (and Amiables, who are the other people-directed Social Styles group) is that they are looking for a little warmth in their relationships. See the chart on page 111 for ways to create it.

It is difficult to influence people-directed customers if you come across as cold or impersonal, but it's also important not to overdo the personal connections. Some restraint in the way you express your feelings will reflect your ability to handle feelings in a mature, professional manner. Being too reserved or focusing excessively on the facts, however, can make you appear unwilling or unable to understand the

Checklist for Modifying Behaviors toward Expressives

Try . . .	Avoid . . .
Planning interaction that supports their dreams and intentions.	Addressing the logic, feasibility, or practical implementation of their ideas.
Leaving time for relating and socializing.	Being curt, cold or reserved.
Talking about their goals and other people's ideas they find stimulating.	Presenting facts and figures, alternatives and abstractions.
Providing few details and instead suggesting ways to achieve their goals.	Contradicting their vision or not implementing their decisions.
Asking for their opinions and ideas about people.	Wasting time being impersonal or judgmental.
Taking enough time to discuss their ideas and views.	Kidding around too much, or "sticking to the agenda" too diligently.
Providing testimonials from people they consider prominent and important.	Talking down to them or providing too much detail.
Offering special, immediate, and personal incentives.	Being dogmatic or prescriptive.
Supporting the individual and his or her ideas.	Supporting just the facts.

Actions for Being More Tell-Directed on the Assertiveness Scale	
Get to the point	Simplify and clarify your opinions. Don't be vague or ambiguous in an effort to be tactful. Say what you mean. Be clear where you stand.
Volunteer information	Don't wait for others to take the lead. Express your opinions.
Be willing to disagree	Don't worry about conflicting with your customer's point of view. It's okay to disagree, as long as you do it without getting defensive or letting the challenge become personal.
Act on your convictions	Take a stand. Make decisions quickly.
Initiate conversation	Take the lead on introducing ideas and solutions.

emotional issues that are important to Expressives and influence their decisions. To help personalize your contacts with Expressives:

- *Verbalize your feelings.* Talk openly about how you feel about the issues you're handling with Expressives. You can establish better relationships by acknowledging your honest reactions. If you are upset, let that be known. Likewise, let it show when you are enthusiastic or excited about where you are headed.

- *Pay personal compliments.* Sincere, legitimate compliments are always welcome by Expressives. Don't hesitate to express these kinds of positive sentiments, or to find other more indirect ways to say good things about your customers. For example, remember their birthdays, write them personal notes, or inquire about family members or the important things they do outside of their professional lives.

- *Be willing to spend time on personal relationships.* Learn to pay attention to the feeling side of human nature. You may not always see an immediate, direct connection between personal involvement with your Expressive customers and achieving sales or other business goals, but friendship and sensitivity to the feelings of others can enrich relationships and build feelings of loyalty and cooperation with Expressives. It can pay off to let your personal feelings enter into a professional relationship in a balanced, appropriate way.

- *Make small talk. Socialize.* Expressives don't want all their communication with you to be "strictly business." Always keep your conversations ultimately focused on your strategic goals and objectives, but mix in bits of conversation that have nothing to do with business.

Expressives are also tell-directed on the assertiveness scale. The chart on page 127 summarizes some of the key actions you can take to modify your behavior to accommodate this preference. The main strategy: Fewer questions, more answers. Tell more often. Ask less often.

UNDERSTANDING AND HANDLING BACK-UP BEHAVIOR WITH EXPRESSIVES

The first instinct for Expressives under tension about a sales situation gone wrong is to fight. When they reach the point of Back-Up, it first shows as Attacking Behaviors.

Expressives in Back-Up manage their tension by trying to control the situation using emotions and feelings. Their strengths can refocus on negatives, sometimes making others very uncomfortable. Their interest in creating excitement with people can change into a personal and public attack. Their affinity for making others feel good can shift into a unsettling ability to make others feel at fault. And their natural preference to reinforce others when things are going well can become an uncanny talent for probing others' vulnerabilities.

An Expressive in the first stage of Back-Up is thinking, "You, your project, your ideas, and your recommendations are *ridiculous*. What are you thinking? What was *I* thinking when I let this process get this far?"

The sooner you begin to *neutralize* Expressives in Back-Up by letting them vent, of course, the more likely you are to be able to recover the relationship. To adapt the LSCPA tool for this purpose, refer back to pages 41 through 44.

Remember, although angry Expressives will at times be unwilling to talk or to share their feelings, remember that tell-directed, people-directed customers ultimately want to connect with you on a personal level. They want to speak, and they want you to listen – closely.

SUMMARY

- Expressives are tell- and people-directed. They are energetic, intuitive, talkative, enthusiastic, ambitious risk-takers. They move fast, energize others, appreciate recognition and visibility, and are misperceived as flighty and not businesslike or task-oriented.

- They expect you to listen, be open, be flexible about time, think of "the big picture," collaborate, and like it when you value their ideas.

- In Relating, the trust-building stage, quickly earn credibility with stories of mutual acquaintances, exclusive information, shared feelings, and endorsement for their energy and vision.

- In Discovering, the problem-defining stage, use your questioning skills to define the goals and the problems you will tackle together. Innovation and risk-taking may very likely be part of the solution.

- In Advocating, when you are aligning the customer toward a solution, use an Expressive's own words and ideas. Make him or her and the solution feel special. Don't drown in detail or options, and don't rush the discussion or act reserved.

- In Supporting the process, take lots of personal responsibility, handle details and the implementation team yourself. Celebrate, look beyond this project to future successes, and expand the scope of your work together.

- Expressives in Back-Up adopt Attacking behavior, the fight response. They try to control the situation and feelings. Neutralize tension by drawing feelings out fully before rectifing the situation.

8 | Lessons from Experts in Versatile Selling

Force is all-conquering,
but its victories are short-lived.
ABRAHAM LINCOLN

You've been through this moment before. After three or four intense days of a workshop, you're approaching the end. You're full of new learning, a bit exhausted and overwhelmed by it all, yet eager to get going and try your new tools and techniques. Often, before the final goodbyes, there's time for sharing what each person thinks are the most important "take aways" – their own key learning. In this chapter you'll get a taste of that experience as it relates to real people using Versatility in their lives.

DON'T BE A CHAMELEON

W. Jacques (Jake) Gibbs has been a self-improvement junkie throughout his 30-plus-year career in investment advising – attending seminars, reading books and cornering experts at every opportunity to ask them questions. However, he looks back from the vantage point of a very successful and ongoing career and says his first exposure to the concepts of *Versatile Selling* laid the foundation of his success.

He was in his early 20s. He was eager, focused, enthusiastic, and, as he later realized, a bit off track.

"I was working hard. I was married, with one kid and another one on the way. I wanted to take care of my family. I was very task driven. My tendency in those days was to try to close deals as fast as I could. I really believed in the value of what I had to offer, so I couldn't see why customers didn't understand that value as clearly as I did.

"But I was turning people off. I didn't understand you couldn't just 'go for the throat.'"

Jacques says he was more driven to succeed than ever after his first exposure to *Versatile Selling* concepts and tools, but he had to come to new insights into the value of adjusting his behaviors – being versatile – to make his sales process more "user friendly" for his customers.

"I figured out I could be more efficient and more effective by not always being so aggressive."

Versatility is all about modifying your behavior, sometimes only ever so slightly, sometimes more significantly. But it's not about being untrue to who you are.

"Integrity," says Jacques, "is the key word."

When he was "going for the throat" early in his sales career, Jacques says, he tended to undervalue people, including himself. He learned the importance of taking time to understand his customers' true needs, as well as his own, and determined to make the satisfaction of those needs the purpose and measure of his work. Based on his experience, he says, it is integrity and strong relationships that create satisfied customers – and personal sales success – not cleverness or manipulation.

"So, if you are an Expressive be an Expressive. If you are a Driver be a Driver. You can make slight modifications in your behavior, stay true to who you are, and get dramatically different results."

Versatility centers on modifying your behavior, not changing who you are as a person. But you have to remain sincere, or most people will worry about your true intentions. You must have in mind the best interests of your customers, and be committed to providing excellent quality and service. If you are only in sales for the money, and that clouds your ability to empathize, serve, respond, and interact honestly with customers, your success will be limited.

KEEP THE FUNNEL FULL

One of the most effective ways to develop the endurance sometimes needed when selling to Amiables and Analyticals (those very deliberate decision-makers), Jacques suggests, is to make sure you are working with plenty of prospects at all times. "Meet lots of people," he says. "Drivers will make decisions quickly. Amiables and Analyticals will take longer. If you have lots of activity it will help you avoid pushing the people who need more time to make up their minds."

LOOK FOR THE LITTLE THINGS

Modify. Don't overhaul. "Regardless of your own style," Jacques suggests, "listen and watch for the little things. How fast they speak. Their expressions. Match yours to theirs. Watch for patterns in their behavior and mimic them in small ways."

VERSATILITY ISN'T ONLY ONE-ON-ONE

Life in sales might be a lot simpler if most transactions involved only you – the salesperson – and a single buyer. That scenario, however, is increasingly rare. There are influencers and stakeholders and co-decision-makers and gatekeepers around every corner, which means, of course, you must be able to adapt to the behavior styles of many people at once. *Versatile Selling,* although relatively simple in theory, can be a complex exercise.

Tom Kramlinger, senior design consultant at Wilson Learning, has learned this lesson repeatedly in his work with Wilson Learning's clients around the world. One recent situation involved a new business opportunity with an existing customer, a major US bank.

"We were already established as an approved provider for the bank. We had gone through a grueling qualification process that required everyone involved in the sales process to bend to the extreme Analytical end of the spectrum. There had been lots of detailed questions in the initial request for proposals, and there were several rounds of follow-up presentations. After several successful implementations, a new opportunity arose for us in the company's electronic banking division. My role was to support our distributor handling the account. We'll call her Gloria. She is an Expressive.

"Gloria had built an excellent relationship at the bank with Terri, a fellow Expressive who was a key influencer in purchase decisions. Gloria enlisted Terri as an ally and advocate to purchase our educational service for the electronic banking group. Part of the benefit we emphasized for Terri was that she would get to deliver our program. We were offering to help make her a 'star' in front of her peers. As an Expressive, she found that very appealing.

"The problem, however, was that Terri was only an influencer, not the decision-maker. Her boss, Byron, controlled the purse strings. I never met him so I can't say for sure if he is a Driver or an Analytical, but Terri's descriptions of his behavior made it clear to us he was a task-directed person. Terri and Gloria both made it clear we would have to demonstrate bottom-line payoff to win the business from him. We decided to treat him primarily as a Driver with an Analytical bent.

"Our strategy was to demonstrate to him how our service would positively influence all the business metrics for which he was responsible.

"We did that. And it worked. But getting the information we needed from Terri was a real challenge. Gloria and I interviewed her several times to find out which metrics mattered most to Byron, and to determine the existing baseline data.

"This research was definitely out of Terri's comfort zone. She was very smart. She could tell us all the theory related to the division's operations, but she didn't know exactly what Byron looked at to measure performance and success. She didn't know the numbers.

"We asked her to see if she could get more details for us. She sent me several e-mails in response. In each one, she sent one of two 'estimated numbers' and some quotes from managers in the department endorsing the need for what we were offering. Clearly, it was easier for her to get opinions than numbers.

"In the end we got enough data to make our case. We wrote up the quotes as 'additional data' to support the decision to buy. And we won the business.

"The lesson in this story is that many different Social Styles can play roles in an account or a sales campaign. Gloria's expressiveness was very helpful in relating to Terri. I shared a lot of feelings with her, too. Then we all had to shift our style in order to meet Byron's needs. And, since Terri was not acquainted with Social Styles and Versatility, Gloria and I had to make an extra effort to adapt to her as an Expressive while at the same time asking her to do things outside of her comfort zone.

"You need Versatility up and down the line, with all your customers, all your allies, all the time."

DIVIDE AND CONQUER —
INDIVIDUALIZE WHEN SELLING TO TEAMS

Hans Fenner also found his Versatility tested by a sale he was making to a team of three people in a billion-dollar division of an international chemical company. Hans is founder and owner of Capita-Consulting in Stuttgart, Germany. In this situation, he found catering to them individually and then bringing them back together was the best way to move everybody to "Yes" in the end.

"The head of the department was a Driver. His two sales directors, both doctors of chemistry, were Analyticals. It was not a problem for me to identify and adapt to their individual preferences, needs, and expectations related to their social styles on a one-to-one basis, but there was a problem during meetings when all three of them were in the same room. It was a challenge to manage all the agenda items smoothly enough to get the three of them all aligned. They seemed to have a good working relationship, but there were some acceptance problems between them because of their style differences.

"I considered concentrating primarily on the needs of the department head, a Driver like me, assuming he was the primary decision maker. But I knew there was a risk in not being sensitive to the needs of the Analytical sales directors. I knew they would have significant impact on the final decision.

"So I persuaded them to meet with me individually, suggesting it would save each of them time if we focused separately on each of their concerns and interests.

"When I prepared a proposal summarizing what had been shared during the individual meetings, I knew I would have to provide a quick summary for the Driver and detailed and precise information for the Analyticals. I did both, developing a two-page cover document and a 20-page attachment. That way I met both sets of needs without confrontation."

COMPANIES HAVE SOCIAL STYLES, TOO

Cyndi Walsh learned early on that companies often have their own predominant Social Styles. "In those situations," she says, "working carefully on key client relationships is a must, not only in understanding how to vary your sales approach but in how to manage your implementation strategy as well."

Cyndi is an account manager and performance consultant for Wilson Learning partner company McCourt Associates. She learned the value of this Social Styles application on company styles working with a long-term client, Linda, while Linda worked at two distinctly different organizations.

"The first company, a large bottled water company, was filled with 'go-getters.' There was heavy competition when it came to getting ideas expressed," Cyndi says. "When people had great ideas, they ran with them. If you weren't in the fast lane you would probably get run over. In order to be heard, everyone – including Linda and I – had to move fast, make quick decisions and be tell-directed."

In this situation, Cyndi was selling and implementing Social Styles and Versatile Salesperson training and education. Based on her assessment of the company's style, she knew it would be critical to quickly find as many ways as possible to make the concepts in those Wilson Learning programs a widespread part of the organization's culture.

"The initial training took off like wildfire. People from all levels of the organization participated, including the executive team. They saw right away that this thinking explained why they were the way they were — and why they didn't click with some people and what they needed to do to overcome potential communication barriers with co-workers and customers. To make sure the concepts and practices were really applied, Linda and I integrated Social Style and Versatile Sales-person techniques everywhere we could."

Moving quickly and being result oriented with this group, Cyndi says, was essential to the acceptance and usefulness of the training.

By contrast, Cyndi and Linda's next project together required a much slower approach.

"Linda had moved on to a large media company with a very ask-directed culture. As a result of understanding the power of Social Styles and Versatility, Linda spent her first few weeks watching, to understand the individual and organizational styles. She figured out she needed to modify her tell-directed approach, which was comfortable for her and had worked so well with the first company. She adapted her behaviors, speaking more slowly, listening, and encouraging others to do the talking. She asked more questions and shared opinions in relation to the responses she heard."

In time, Linda developed her skills in the various question types we've seen in Chapter 2: permission questions, fact-finding questions, feeling-finding questions, best-least questions, magic wand questions, tell-me-more questions, catch-all questions. People throughout the new company complimented Linda on her ability to synthesize information, Cyndi says, and for her knack of always seeming to have something important to say whenever she spoke.

"Her transition to the new company culture was complete, although after a day of being versatile at work, she says she goes home and moves back to her own comfort zone, bossing everyone around."

SOMETIMES YOU NEED TO BE
VERSATILE AT A MOMENT'S NOTICE

Thomas Koven's sales manager asked him to make a presentation to a client he had never met about one of his company's key products. Thomas, an instructional designer, facilitator and consultant, says things didn't get off to a very good start.

"I arrived at the customer's site 15 minutes early and was ushered into a conference room to set up my handouts and slides. The room was a mess. All the tables and chairs had been piled haphazardly in one corner. I stood there in a state of shock wondering how I was ever going to make a respectable presentation in the midst of this chaos."

Rather than getting angry, he got busy.

"I took off my suit jacket and got down to work, pulling the tables and chairs into a semblance of order. Approximately five minutes before our scheduled start time and at the height of my fevered efforts, the door to the room opened and a man I assumed to be my client stuck in his head and said, 'How much more time do you need?'

"I thought to myself, 'What is this? No, 'Hi how are you?' No introduction? This guy has as much interpersonal skill as a doorknob.' But then I got a grip on the situation. Instead of reacting negatively I said to myself, 'Hold on, Thomas. What is this guy telling you about the way he likes to do business? Hmm, let's see. Concerned about time. Fast paced. No relationship building. Sounds like a Driver to me.'

"I walked up to the client, looked him directly in the eyes, stuck out my hand and said, 'Good morning. My name is Thomas and I need five more minutes.'

"Without missing a beat, he responded, 'I'm Robert, and you've got your five minutes.' And with that he disappeared through the doorway.

"I made sure I was ready because I knew that precisely five minutes later, Robert and his team would be walking in the door. They did. They sat around the table, took out their pens and pads, and looked at me, waiting. And I was ready. I knew exactly what would happen next.

I waited, and right on cue, Robert looked up from some papers he was handling and said, 'How long is this going to take?'

"I said, 'Thanks for inviting me here, Robert. I understand that we are scheduled for 90 minutes today, but I am going to get you out of here in 60.'

"He said. 'That's great.'"

The sales call started off poorly, but once Thomas decided to do what needed to be done, and then fought off the instinctive, habitual reaction to his first impressions of this new client, things went well.

"The presentation was a breeze, and closing the business was not a problem either. After I packed up, Robert walked me out to the reception area. As we walked we talked, and he was focused on implementation – but not of the project I had just presented. He wanted to talk about the next project he wanted to do with us. In his mind, the current piece of business was a done deal. His real energy was already focused on the next piece. No invitation to sit down or come back to his office. We stood talking by the front door."

As he walked to his car, Thomas says, he realized that his composure (not getting flustered by the disarray in the room), and his Versatility (picking up and adjusting quickly to the client's Driver style, promising to be ready in five minutes and then offering to finish his presentation in 60 minutes instead of 90) had paid off well. "I realized I had closed two pieces of business that day in approximately 30 seconds – the first 30 seconds of the meeting."

YOU CAN ALWAYS BECOME MORE VERSATILE

Nic Hallett is the performance development manager for The Excel Communications Group in the United Kingdom. He always prided himself in being – or at least wanting to be – empathetic and attuned to the needs and feelings of others, but struggled with some relationships nonetheless. His relationship with a senior manager who was one of his key customers is a perfect example.

"Whenever I wandered past her neat, minimalist office, she would be there in a formal business suit, looking serious, working quietly. I would think to myself, 'Poor, sad person.' And then I would bounce in to try to cheer her up. But a smile and a joke never worked. So I would say to myself, 'I'll have to try harder.'

"The more I tried the less I succeeded. She started to avoid me; kept me at a distance and looked awkward whenever I was around.

"Around that time I took a workshop on Versatility in sales. We discussed the differences between Analyticals and Expressives. And the light went on.

"The next time I had a chance, I politely knocked on her door. I waited quietly for her to finish what she was doing. When she looked up I said, in soft, measured tones, that I had been giving some thought to an issue that was likely to be coming up for her.

"She welcomed my ideas. She smiled. We talked. And we still do."

Nic's conscious change of behavior, of course, is the whole point of *Versatile Selling,* and it is reinforced over and over again on this individual level, as well as on a much broader scale. It's never too late to be Versatile.

BIG MOVES TOWARD VERSATILITY
START WITH SMALL STEPS

In Colombia, Maria Teresa de Vergara and Dr. Alberto Perez La Rotta have been involved in helping 3,500 sales and client service employees learn and practice Versatility at Bancolombia, the country's largest private bank. Maria Teresa is general manager and a senior consultant for Wilson Learning Andina y Rio de la Plata in Colombia and Alberto is president. The group has local offices in Mexico, Colombia, Peru, Argentina, Brazil and in Orlando, Florida in the US.

Bancolombia, she says, is striving for – and is actually achieving – a significant change in the culture of the organization. The employees want to build better client relationships across the entire organization, and ultimately they are doing it one customer encounter at a time. The broad success, she says, shows up in small stories like these being told by people of different social styles throughout Bancolombia, more and more frequently:

> "I am a Driver. I like to have control of my time and to be very efficient with my day-to-day activities. I have always been very concerned with client satisfaction and tried to be as prepared as possible to meet my customers' needs. One of the first times I put Versatility into practice was with an Expressive client. He was very outgoing, but I didn't give him much opportunity to explain himself before I offered him a family money management program that I had prepared to talk about with him. As I listened, I realized he had come in expecting to purchase a more high-tech, integrated product. I modified my style. We talked through the big-picture benefits of what I was offering, clarified his needs and expectations, agreed on a best fit, and signed a policy."

> "I have an Amiable Social Style. I like having strong relationships, and I want to bond with and earn acceptance from the people I work with. I had the chance to work with an Analytical customer after my training. He was reserved and asked only a few questions, mostly focused on cost and specific product details. I was glad I had prepared answers to all the specific questions that might be asked about the features and benefits of the products we agreed to discuss. I also knew I would have to be cautious and give him time and space to understand the benefits of the product. It took some extensive thought, and effort, but he became a client."

> "I am an Expressive. I was meeting with an Analytical client and, in my usual style, rushed enthusiastically into the sales process. It wasn't long before I realized that I had to be a bit more cautious and present my case with less enthusiasm and more

facts, in a chronological format. I realized this client needed pre-cise data and then time to think carefully before finally making a decision. In the end, he was very satisfied and specifically thanked the bank for the 'detailed consultation.'"

"I am an Analytical. I usually work behind the scenes to sup-port the sales teams, helping them assess the risk and opportu-nity of big deals. I know my love of facts and analysis can bore the Expressives we have out there selling. So I try to give them big, colorful headlines and try to inject a little 'accounting hu-mor' here and there when I make my presentations. I figure that even if they laugh at me more than they do at my jokes, it's worth it to get my points across and capture their attention. We actu-ally enjoy our differences and appreciate what each Style con-tributes."

VERSATILITY PAYS OFF IN DOCUMENTS

Michael Leimbach, a vice president at Wilson Learning, suggests prac-ticing what he calls Versatility Jujitsu. Jujitsu is the art of finding a way to leverage your weaknesses into strengths.

In writing letters and e-mails, Michael says, "My natural Analytical tendency is to structure documents in a logical sequence – it just feels right that way. I begin with the background, move to the major points, and end with my conclusion or recommendation. Several years ago, when working with a challenging Driver client, I hit upon a new tech-nique. When writing letters or e-mails to this client, I would compose my document as I normally do (for my own comfort). Then I would in-vert it. I would move the last paragraph or sentences, which always contained my reasoned conclusion, to the top of the document. Then I would move my opening paragraphs or sentences, which contained the details, to the end. A brief edit would smooth things out. That way, my Driver client could quickly see our recommendation, yet skip the details at the end if she wanted to. I have found that this works with both of the Tell-Assertive styles, Drivers and Expressives.

"There are many ways people can use their own style strengths to help them modify their behavior. Probably because I'm an Analytical, I am very diligent about always having my computer do an automatic spell check on my documents as the last thing I do before I send out any written messages or documents. Now, before I run the spell check, I automatically do a 'Style Check.' First I ask myself what style my reader is. Then, for example, I ask myself questions like these:

- Is this too long for a Driver or an Expressive?
- Did I begin this e-mail with a personal connection if the reader is an Amiable or Expressive?
- Did I use enough expressive words to describe things I'm excited about, for an Amiable or Expressive?

"Now, if I could just figure out how to program my computer to do this automatically. . . ."

STEADY THE COURSE WHEN WORKING WITH EXPRESSIVES

Page Glasgow, a consultant with Page Glasgow and Associates, a Wilson Learning partner company in Troy, Michigan, in the US, has experienced the ups and downs of working with Expressives.

"I was working with an Expressive who was looking at using our sales curriculum. After our presentation, he said, 'Wow! I think we will use everything you offered.'

"I knew there was no competition on this deal, so I felt pretty good about getting the business. After a subsequent presentation to the sales executives in this company, they seemed to me to be impressed but noncommittal. My contact reported that they loved it. 'Give me some pricing and we'll set up the seminars,' he said.

"After I gave him the pricing, he wrote me, 'The sales guys have sticker shock. They think we should look somewhere else.' Naturally my spirits fell. But soon, he came back with a new tactic. 'I'll meet with them individually to see where they are."

"When he completed that cycle, he called me and said, 'Work with me on prices for a pilot project this year, and if they go well, I'm sure we'll roll it out later.'

"What did I learn? Expressives can be all over the map, sometimes on your side, sometimes moving away. They are not naturally inclined to think through budgets and other ramifications of decisions. It has turned out to be a good account, but I learned not to get caught up in my Expressive's enthusiasm and to ask reality-based questions such as, 'In view of your budget problems, is this really going to fly?' This has to be done in a friendly way, guiding them to their decision while injecting reality as you move forward. But it certainly can pay off."

VERSATILITY HELPS YOU APPRECIATE DIFFERENCES

Laura Campos and her team at Wilson Learning Andina's office in Mexico have been working with a large pharmaceutical firm to train 1,000 sales representatives and 100 managers in Versatility. One client, an Expressive, told her, "Before I understood what it means to be a Driver I used to think of these kinds of people as difficult customers. I would do everything I could to avoid visiting them. Now I understand and respect their fast-to-task orientation and have been able to do more effective calls with them."

Another of Laura's clients, a Driver manager, was guilty of "pushing all my sales team solely for results, being harshly direct with them, and not having much patience for their points of view." That manager now realizes, Laura says, that Versatility is as important in coaching and supervising as it is in selling. The manager said after the training, "This has increased my comfort in sharing expectations and needs differently with different people, but it has also proven a great opportunity for me to model the Versatility the sales reps need to demonstrate with our customers."

It's quite easy to see the huge bottom-line potential of having 3,500 sales and service people in one organization focused on applying the lessons of *Versatile Selling,* as the employees at Bancolombia are doing. It's also easy to see the difference that adapting behavior to make customers comfortable can make on an individual level. Think of Jacques Gibbs' life- and career-changing experience.

What's not always so easy, however, is overcoming that instinctive desire to communicate, relate, and sell in the ways in which we ourselves are most comfortable.

The true power of Versatility is *applying* what you now know, not just knowing what you know. Habits don't die easily. Laura's Expressive client, for example, is going to have days when facing Drivers will once again feel daunting and painful. Her newly enlightened Driver manager will have high-pressure moments when all the newfound patience for dealing with the diverse Social Styles in the sales team will disappear. The same will be true for you. The impulse to do things the way you have always done things will probably never go away. As we've seen, habits are hard to change. You are certain to find yourself in situations in which you will realize you have inadvertently, or perhaps even deliberately, lapsed into comfortable, habitual but unproductive behaviors.

It may be challenging at times to implement what you've learned in reading *Versatile Selling,* but your persistence and your efforts will pay off. Be aware – of your own behavior and that of others. Be yourself, but be versatile.

Our hope is that we've focused a bit of light on behaviors that can help you move more of your customers to "Yes!" Once you see it, don't close your eyes. It is shining along the path to more success in sales.

Appendix

Social Style Summary

Use this chart to refresh yourself before you communicate with customers. If you do so repeatedly, a great deal of the content will become habitual for you and your Versatility will steadily improve.

	ANALYTICAL	AMIABLE	DRIVER	EXPRESSIVE
PRIMARY ASSET	Systematic	Supportive	Focused	Energizing
BACK-UP BEHAVIOR	Avoid	Acquiesce	Autocratic	Attach
FOR GROWTH NEEDS TO	Decide	Initiate	Listen	Check
STRONGEST PERSONAL MOTIVATOR	Respect	Approval	Results	Recognition
NEEDS CLIMATE THAT	Describes	Supports	Commits	Collaborates
LET THEM SAVE	Face	Relationships	Time	Effort
MAKE EFFORT TO BE	Accurate	Agreeable	Efficient	Stimulating
SUPPORT THEIR	Principles and thinking	Relationships and feelings	Conclusions and actions	Visions and intuitions
STRESS BENE-FITS THAT ANSWER	HOW problem is solved	WHY solution is best	WHAT solution will do	WHO else has used
FOR DECISIONS GIVE THEM	Data and evidence	Assurances and guarantees	Options and probabilities	Testimony and incentives
FOLLOW UP WITH	Service	Support	Action	Attention

Guidelines for Social Style Identification

You will find it easier if you try to identify a person's Social Style if you observe one dimension – Ask-Tell Assertiveness or Task-People Responsiveness – at a time.

ANALYTICAL

- Reserved or composed posture
- Actions controlled or careful
- Wants facts or details
- Serious gaze
- Minimal gestures
- Limited facial expression
- Little sharing of feelings, personal information or storytelling

DRIVER

Task-Directed Responsiveness

- Seldom uses voice to emphasize
- Quiet and indirect
- Deliberate, studied, or slow-paced
- Ask questions more often than makes statements
- Tends to lean backward

Ask-Directed Assertiveness

Tell-Directed Assertiveness

- Uses voice to emphasize details
- Loud, clear, and direct
- Makes statements more often than asks questions
- Tends to lean forward

People-Directed Responsiveness

AMIABLE

- Relaxed posture
- Actions open or eager
- Wants acknowledgment or support
- Friendly gaze, varied gestures
- Animated facial expressions
- Shares feelings, tells stories, reveals personal information
- Limited talk of facts
- Focused on relationship issues

EXPRESSIVE

Social Style Modification Strategies

If you have identified your customer's Social Style, then this table will help you adapt your behavior to your customer's comfort zone. Check the strategies that form the borders of your customer's type and use them to shape your behavior when working with this person.

ANALYTICAL

- Talk about the task; reference facts as well as feelings
- Try to organize your thoughts in a logical pattern when communicating
- Acknowledge the ideas and points that others make
- Articulate expected results of taking action

DRIVER

Increasing Task-Directed Responsiveness

- Be open to others' opinions, concerns and feelings
- Acknowledge the value you place on other people's time
- Demonstrate a willingness to follow the lead of others
- Ask for cooperation, but don't demand it

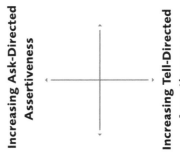

- Demonstrate a willingness to get to the point
- Volunteer information you have to others
- Be willing to express points of disagreement
- Summarize the positions you feel others are suggesting

Increasing People-Directed Responsiveness

AMIABLE

- Take the time to establish rapport with your co-workers
- Reinforce other people when they express good ideas
- Share your feelings or personal information
- Allow yourself and others to break the routine while problem solving

EXPRESSIVE

Resources

IF YOU'D LIKE TO LEARN MORE ABOUT VERSATILE SELLING SKILLS

Managing Interpersonal Relations, the program that pioneered Versatility techniques, was developed by Wilson Learning in the early 1970s. Ongoing refinement has led to the current program, *The Versatile Salesperson*. With more than a million graduates worldwide, Versatility is a proven asset to any sales process.

The Versatile Salesperson is available for both classroom and e-learning environments. A suite of tools supports ongoing learning with specialized planning checklists, advisory guidelines, a manager's tool kit, a CD-ROM reinforcement program, and other resources. A specially adapted version for the pharmaceutical industry, *The Versatile Pharmaceutical Representative*, has just been released.

The program is used by organizations of all sizes and in a wide range of business and non-profit sectors. Culturally adapted translations are available in 19 dialects and languages. In addition to the pharmaceutical industry program, custom versions for salespeople and sales managers in the health care, retail, travel and leisure, automotive, high tech, IT, manufacturing, financial, insurance, capital equipment and other industries are also available. Find out more about *The Versatile Salesperson* and Wilson Learning locations by visiting the Wilson Learning website at www.wilsonlearning.com.

"If there is one factor that differentiates high performing salespeople, it is Versatility – the ability to adapt one's approach and style of communication to meet the personal needs and expectations of the customer. Every salesperson will acknowledge that their selling skills work better with some customers than with others. The skills in The Versatile Salesperson *help salespeople adapt to all types of customers and help ensure success."*

Ron Remillard, Director of the Sales Training and Development Institute,

Georgia Pacific Corporation

IF YOU'D LIKE TO LEARN MORE
ABOUT COUNSELOR SELLING SKILLS

Wilson Learning began offering Sales Sonics, the predecessor to *The Counselor Salesperson* program, in 1965. The program has undergone continuous revision, local adaptation and customization ever since. To date, more than a million participants around the world have learned the Counselor mindset and skills presented in this program, in both classroom and e-learning environments.

Organizations of all sizes and in a wide range of business and non-profit sectors use this program. Culturally adapted translations are available in 19 dialects and languages. Custom versions for salespeople and sales managers in the pharmaceutical, health care, retail, travel and leisure, automotive, high tech, IT, manufacturing, financial, insurance, capital equipment and other industries are also available. Find out more about *The Counselor Salesperson* and Wilson Learning locations by visiting the Wilson Learning website at www.wilsonlearning.com.

"Wilson Learning played a critical role in the reinvention of our sales force and our clients' perception of our value."

Ron DeLio, Chief Operating Officer,
Strategic Travel Solutions Division, Rosenbluth International

"We've used the Counselor method for more than 20 years and have thousands of graduates of the course. Our mission is 'To be the best in the eyes of our customers, employees and shareholders,' which means 'Do what's right,' 'Do the best you can,' and 'Help customers, employees and shareholders get what they want.' The Counselor method has been and continues to be the CORE of our way of accomplishing our mission."

Ed Gilbertson, Manager, Sales & Management Training, TRANE,
An American Standard Company

"These Wilson Learning methods are 'how we do business.' They are what sets us apart from our competitors and the reason why our customers rate us more highly in customer satisfaction than our peers. In the Counselor method we have discovered the sales system solution that delivers on our customers' needs."

Paul Bryant, Senior Manager,
Financial Services, Suncorp Metway Ltd.

THE WILSON LEARNING LIBRARY

Win-Win Selling, The Original 4-Step Counselor Approach for Building Long-Term Relationships with Buyers. Differentiating your company's products and services is a big challenge today. But a company's sales force can become a significant differentiator, and gain sustainable advantages, if it adopts the Counselor approach. A win-win mind and skill set, based on trust, problem-solving and side-by-side work between seller and customer, makes buying easy. And because the seller stays by the customer after the sale, the door opens for long-term, expanding business.

Fortune 500 global and other companies in 30 countries have used Wilson Learning's Counselor approach for years with astonishing success. The book gives the million-plus people who have taken Wilson Learning's *The Counselor Salesperson* course a refresher, and gives others a powerful sales process. Larry Wilson, author of *One Minute Salesperson* and founder of Wilson Learning (1965) wrote the foreword to the book. It's indispensable for salespeople and sales managers, who say it's solid, practical and really works.

"The Counselor Approach enhanced our leadership position by helping our sales and marketing organization discover what is most important in our marketplace. As a result, we are adding more value to our customers as a means of advocating for the patient."

Dan Schlewitz, Vice President Sales,
Medtronic CRM

Win-Win Selling (ISBN 90-77256-01-6)
160 pages, 160 X 230 cm (6" x 9"), softcover with flaps
Models, charts, anecdotes, an index and other resources.
To locate shops and services selling this book visit www.novavistapub.com.

The Social Styles Handbook. Backed by a database profiling more than 2 million people, Wilson Learning's Social Styles concepts are powerful, life-changing communication tools. The ways people prefer to influence others and how they feel about showing emotion identify them as Analyticals, Expressives, Drivers or Amiables. You feel comfortable acting within your own style. But to relate well with others, you must consciously adjust your style to the styles of others. That is the principal of Versatility, which improves performance in every aspect of your work and personal life.

Find your style and learn to recognize others'. Understand and appreciate strengths and differences in each. Learn how to adapt your behavior – become Versatile – while still being yourself. Important tools for recognizing rising tension in Back-Up Behavior and handling it productively, plus techniques for influencing others to make change and progress, make this a strong, proven approach. It helps people make sense and take a nonjudgmental approach to our diverse world.

"The concepts in this book changed my career and my life. I've been through a lot of training, and even after 33 years in sales I try to keep learning. Social Styles, Versatility and the Wilson Learning approach to sales have given me the solid foundation I needed to achieve the success I've had."

W. Jacques Gibbs, Investment Advisor

The Social Style Handbook (ISBN 90-77256-04-0)
160 pages, 160 X 230 cm (6" x 9"), softcover with flaps
Models, charts, anecdotes, an index and other resources.
To locate shops and services selling this book, visit www.novavistapub.com.

Contributors

ABOUT THE AUTHORS

Thomas Koven, B.A., lives in Canada and is a proud member of Wilson Learning's Extended Enterprise, a dedicated network of certified facilitators and designers across the world. Thomas believes that the success of a business is founded on the success of its people. He has used this simple principle to produce improved performance for Wilson Learning clients throughout North America, Latin America and Asia. He has contributed to the development of many of Wilson Learning's blended offerings and is the lead designer and writer of Wilson Learning's latest update for *The Versatile Salesperson* progam.

Tom Kramlinger, Ph.D., is Senior Design Consultant at Wilson Learning. During his 28 years with the company, he has designed programs in sales and sales management and researched and designed special applications for clients in the capital equipment, financial, automotive, transport, chemical, IT, insurance and telecommunication industries. He taught *The Counselor Salesperson* pilot program in Japan and collaborated on its cultural adaptation there. His current focus is on creating and communicating advanced solutions for Fortune 500 global clients that integrate Wilson Learning technologies.

Michael Leimbach, Ph.D., is Vice President, Global Research and Development at Wilson Learning. He and his Global R&D team have created the innovative performance improvement systems that make Wilson Learning a leader in human performance improvement. He has been helping organizations gain sales force effectiveness for over 20 years. Michael has been involved with updating and enhancing all of Wilson Learning's sales-effectiveness programs and created Wilson Learning's sales-effectiveness diagnostic capabilities. He has published numerous professional articles and has presented before a wide range of clients and professional organizations around the world.

Ed Tittel, B.A., M.A., is the Portfolio Manager for the Sales and Service offering for Wilson Learning Americas. Ed has over 20 years' experience in the human performance improvement industry and has co-authored several Wilson Learning brand and custom offerings. During his tenure at Wilson Learning, he has consulted with Fortune 100 organizations throughout the United States, Europe and Asia. Prior to his work at Wilson Learning, Ed was a developer and demonstrator for the National Diffusion Network within the United States Department of Education.

David Yesford is the Vice President, Product Marketing for Wilson Learning Worldwide. He has spent 17 years helping organizations develop an understanding of effective consultative sales strategies. David has been involved with creating, updating and customizing sales effectiveness systems and most recently has lead Wilson Learning's effort to launch blended sales effectiveness capabilities. David's primary interest is to ensure that a person's performance improves in ways he or she values and the organization needs.

ABOUT THE PROJECT DEVELOPMENT TEAM

Brian McDermott is a consultant, business writer and editor with extensive experience in the field, particularly in the area of training. **Jane Eddy** has trained and managed sales teams using Versatile Selling techniques in the UK and Australia. **Karien Sticker** is a graphics designer specialized in instructional page design. **Ruth Sleurs** is a graphics designer with a focus on book cover and marketing design. **Andrew Karre** is a technical editor specialized in adult learning materials.

All the authors at Wilson Learning and the Nova Vista Publishing staff wish to thank the team, and others who lent their expertise, for their enthusiasm, dedication and resourcefulness in developing this book.

Index